The City Beneath Us

194+34

The City Beneath Us
Building the New York Subways

New York Transit Museum
with Vivian Heller

W. W. Norton & Company
New York   London

The City Beneath Us
New York Transit Museum with Vivian Heller

page 1: Lafayette Street, Manhattan; IRT Contract 1 line. June 1906.

pages 2–3: Fourth Avenue between 37th and 38th Streets, Brooklyn; BRT Fourth Avenue line. January 1911.

page 5: Near 42nd Street and Lexington Avenue, Manhattan; IRT Lexington Avenue line. July 1919.

page 6: Battery Park, Manhattan; IRT Contract 2 line. December 1903. This image shows the operation of a hydraulic lining erector, which was a traveling platform fitted with an extensible radial arm that would lift a 900-pound cast-iron plate and pivot it into position so that workers could bolt it into place.

The text of this book is composed in Filosophia with the display set in SuperGrotesk.

Book design and composition by Laura Lindgren

Library of Congress Cataloging-in-Publication Data
The city beneath us : building the New York subway / New York Transit Museum with Vivian Heller.

p.   cm.
Includes bibliographical references and index.
ISBN 0-393-05797-6

1. Subways—New York (State)—New York—Design and construc-tion—History. 2. Subways—New York (State)—New York—Design and construction—History. 2. Subways—New York (State)—New York—Design and construction—Pictorial works. I. Heller, Vivian. II. New York Transit Museum.
TF847.N5C52 2004
625.4'2'097471022—dc22

2004054718

W. W. Norton & Company, 500 Fifth Avenue, New York, NY 10110 www.wwnorton.com

W. W. Norton & Company Ltd., Castle House, 75/76 Wells Street, London, WIT 3QT

2 3 4 5 6 7 8 9 0

This book is dedicated to the employees of the New York
City subway system and its predecessor agencies—to those
who built it, those who run it, and those who are passionate
about its future.

—New York Transit Museum

To my husband, Kenji Fujita, whose love and knowledge of
New York City informed every page of this book.

—Vivian Heller

Contents

Preface

With this book, we celebrate the hundred-year anniversary of the New York subway. To mark this occasion, we have dug deep into the archives of the New York Transit Museum, where the history of the New York subway has been carefully preserved in a remarkable collection of historic images.

What do these images tell us? They tell us about an incredible feat of construction. But they tell us even more than that: they document the birth of the thriving metropolis we know today.

The building of the New York subway was the most ambitious civic project of its time, and its success was instantaneous and enduring. At the same time, the subway shared in every major crisis that swept over the city, undergoing cycles of growth, decline, and regeneration.

Decade by decade, the subway has struggled to adapt to the changing needs of the city. The events of 9/11 put the subway through one of its most punishing trials, and yet not a single passenger was hurt. The damage was repaired under budget and ahead of schedule; the indomitable spirit of the first builders was with us again.

A hundred years ago, the subway enabled New York to meet the challenges of a new century. As we enter the twenty-first century, we are once again faced with demands that call for building on a grand scale. The Fulton Street Hub will transform the entire downtown area; the Second Avenue Subway will provide much-needed service along the East Side of Manhattan; the first expansion of the Long Island Rail Road since 1868 will bring thousands of commuters into Grand Central Terminal, giving them access to the East Side; the extension of the 7 line west from Times Square will provide service to an area that is poised for major development.

Once again, the subway is on the move, carrying our great city into the future.

—Peter S. Kalikow
Chairman, Metropolitan Transportation Authority

Acknowledgments

The photos shown in the portfolio section of *The City Beneath Us* are drawn from the collection of the New York Transit Museum. We are grateful to Vivian Heller for examining our vast collection in depth, and for selecting the remarkable images in this book. We also thank her for writing a rich, well-paced, and compelling history of the first hundred years of the subway, giving life to a story many people don't know.

In the course of researching the book, we relied on the vast expertise of many longtime employees of New York City Transit's Department of Subways. Interviews were conducted with (in alphabetical order): Ronald Anderson, Maintenance Supervisor II, Division of Car Equipment; Arthur Bethell, General Superintendent, Maintenance of Way; Edward Brennan, General Superintendent, Division of Car Equipment; John Doherty, Superintendent, Division of Car Equipment; Nathaniel Ford, Chief of Operations, Service Delivery; Joseph Hofmann, former Senior Vice President; Herbert Lambert, Assistant Chief Transportation Officer, Rapid Transit Operations; Michael Landi, Superintendent, Division of Car Equipment; Robert Lobenstein, General Superintendent, Maintenance of Way; Arthur Murphy, Assistant Transit Management Analyst, Division of Car Equipment; Jerry Skinner, Director, Service Delivery and Rail Maintenance, Human Resources; and William Wall, Train Service Supervisor, Rapid Transit Operations.

Sandra Bloodworth, Director, MTA Arts for Transit, provided details of the comeback of the subway in the 1980s and Arts for Transit. Professor Maura Spiegel of Columbia University provided invaluable guidance on historical sources. Daniel Myerson supplied expert advice on the manuscript.

Joseph Cunningham's comments enabled us to accurately caption the images. Lawrence Stelter added much relevant information to the captions, and Joseph Raskin, Assistant Director, Government and Community Relations at New York City Transit, assisted in fact checking.

We appreciate the support of our sister institutions, who provided access to their collections: The Shoreline Trolley Museum Library, the Columbia University Oral History Library, and the Robert F. Wagner Labor Archives at the Tamiment Library at New York University. We also thank Donald W. Harold for providing images from his collection.

The knowledge of Sue Ann Pascucci, former archivist at the New York Transit Museum, and Miriam Tierney steered us through the research process; Senior Curator Charles Sachs skillfully guided final image selection and scrutinized the text through many drafts. Sharon Adams hauled historic materials and proved to be an able archival assistant. Our thanks go to Noah Lukeman for anticipating the Subway Centennial and finding an author and publisher; and to Jim Mairs, Senior Editor at W. W. Norton, for his love of infrastructure and his unerring eye. Laura Lindgren provided an elegant book design, and photographer Anne Day's steady hand reproduced the images in all their splendid clarity.

We are grateful to the Metropolitan Transportation Authority and its agencies for their support of the New York Transit Museum, and for allowing us to preserve and illuminate the important history of New York's public transportation.

—Gabrielle Shubert
Director, New York Transit Museum

The City Beneath Us

CHAPTER ONE

"From City Hall to Harlem in Fifteen Minutes!"

I n a film comedy by Thomas Edison, a man carrying a lunch pail hurries up to a subway kiosk, shakes the hand of a subway official seated just inside the entry, rushes down the steps, leaps down onto the track, lights a stick of dynamite—and is then seen shooting through the subway tunnel, arms outstretched, ribbons of cloth fluttering at his sides. The title of Edison's film is *From City Hall to Harlem in 15 Seconds!*, a parody of New York's rallying cry during the early years of the subway. The desire for speed was an obsession in New York at the turn of the century, perhaps because at that time the city's streets were so choked. Then as now, New Yorkers were in a rush, but it had become increasingly difficult for them to get anywhere.

It was this desperate desire for speed, for circulation, that was finally answered by the Interborough Rapid Transit Company on October 27, 1904, when New Yorkers went "subway mad" over the inauguration of the Interborough Rapid Transit, the most talked-about event in the city

IRT subway inspection tour prior to opening, dignitaries at City Hall station, 1904: Mayor McClellan (center foreground); contractor John B. McDonald (at edge of platform). NYTM (New York Transit Museum)

13

IRT logo, from *Interborough Rapid Transit, The New York Subway: Its Construction and Equipment* (New York: Interborough Rapid Transit Company, 1904). NYTM

since the Civil War. After four trying years of putting up with evacuation orders, propped-up buildings, gutted streets, and a spate of deaths, disasters, and injuries, the day had finally come when New Yorkers could celebrate an event that would change the history of the city forever. But to grasp the full significance of this remarkable day, let's go back to nineteenth-century New York, and to the problems that were plaguing it.

Dark, airless apartments so crowded you couldn't turn around; no running water; one privy per building, all the way down in the yard; no light, no air, no privacy, no space—this was the New York that countless immigrants knew, a city strangled by its own growth. By 1860, New York was the leading port and busiest manufacturing city in the country: between 1850 and 1900, its population increased fivefold. Wave after wave of immigrants appeared, pouring into the twenty-three square miles of Manhattan, with the greatest concentration in lower Manhattan, creating the worst crowding the world has ever seen.

Humanity seemed to sweat out of the buildings, one reporter wrote; wherever you turned, you were confronted with garbage and filth. Cholera, typhus, tuberculosis, yel-

low fever—these were the daily companions of the poor. "Air, give me air!" was the cry from the tenements, a cry no one seemed to hear. The streets were a brawling mess of horse-drawn vehicles of every kind, vehicles moving— or not moving—at different speeds.

There were many reformers who understood from early on that the most direct route to social change lay in urban mass transit, prophets like Rufus Gilbert, a physician who became renowned for his brilliant surgery during the Civil War. After the war was over, Gilbert returned to his native New York, and before long he was working in the tenements. A veteran of battlefields, he was so outraged by what he saw, by the squalor and crowding and suffering and disease, that he vowed to give up his medical career in order to dedicate all his energies to the poor. He was determined to help deliver them from the slums; he began by studying the problem of powering an underground train. Just a few miles to the north lay the wholesome countryside, but for the poor it was galaxies away.

"This is a higher form of service," he wrote to a medical colleague of his, who believed he was making a terrible mistake. "There is no other cure for the misery you and I have seen; with all due respect, everything else seems futile to me."

This great humanist lent his support to another visionary of his times, a politically savvy inventor by the name of Alfred Ely Beach, publisher of *Scientific American* magazine. It was Beach's dream to build a pneumatic (air-driven) subway, but he knew that the corrupt officials of the day would never give him a franchise, so he decided to simply bypass them. He would build a 312-foot subway, a prototype, that would dazzle the city and garner support for the full-scale subway that was his ultimate goal.

Beach rented out the basement of a building on Murray Street and hired a crew of diggers who would work only at night. Since he had no official permission for his plan, the work was carried out in total secrecy. When his diggers came up against the foundations of an old Dutch fort, Beach didn't lose any of his resolve. The stones were removed one by one, and the digging went on as before. Obsessed, Beach would go down into the tunnel to work with the men; the tunnel was the passageway to his life's dream.

During the day, he wrestled with a great worry of his: how would he lure his fellow New Yorkers underground? The underground was associated with fearsome things; and then, like a vision, it came to him. He would bring splendid chandeliers and a grand piano down into his tunnel; he would turn it into an underground palace, a place of subterranean music and light. When it opened in 1870, the *New York Herald* hailed Beach's pneumatic subway as an "Aladdin's cave," and riders were astonished by the magical smoothness of the ride. It was like being aboard a fairy ship, one traveler said; the car floated the 312 feet from Murray to Warren and back again like a feather gliding on the air.

Though Beach succeeded in enchanting the public, he was unable to move New York's corrupt politicians, backed by William Marcy Tweed and Tammany Hall. They

NEW POST OFFICE
& PROPOSED
BROADWAY UNDERGROUND RAILWAY.

made sure that no financial backer could be found. Yet Beach continued to struggle to achieve his goal. Realizing that air propulsion would be less cost-effective than steam, he revised his plan, but then the city was struck by the stock market crash of 1873, and all hopes of raising the money finally died.

What happened to the tunnel? It was rented out, first as a shooting gallery, then as a wine cellar. On some nights, a lone figure could be seen in the vault, strangely boyish despite his white hair, perched on a wine crate, staring into the dark. It was Beach, still dreaming of achieving the impossible.

Years later, the diggers of the Brooklyn Rapid Transit came upon the remains of Beach's endeavor. Sealed up, the waiting room was perfectly preserved, and it had an eerie splendor, astonishing the dazed workers.

The 1880s and 1890s were the age of the els, the elevated lines that were powered by steam locomotives and which carried 115 million people in 1886, twice the entire population of the United States. But for all that, the els were inadequate. A high-speed underground system was desperately needed. The problem of the tenements, of crowding, was worse than ever, and in these years of upheaval and social ferment, when the poor were being pushed ever further into crime and disease, deliverance from the slums was still the rallying cry.

Socialists and anarchists were multiplying on the Lower East Side, captivating huge audiences. Fear began to spread into the gilded salons of the rich: the fear of revolution; the fear of disease—there was always the specter of an epidemic, a plague engulfing the city.

But who would build the subway? Who would finance the outrageously expensive plan, which would cost four times more than an el and twenty times more than a streetcar line? Daunted by this epic task, private entrepreneurs

New post office and proposed Broadway underground railway, 1869, from Alfred Beach *Prospectus*. NYTM

failed to come forward. New Yorkers fought over whether the city should take charge, risking the danger of the kind of corruption and graft that had become the norm under the insatiable Boss Tweed.

It was former mayor Abram Hewitt, an aristocratic-looking man with piercing gray-blue eyes, who finally broke the stalemate crippling the city. Hewitt was a veteran crusader against the corruptions of Tammany Hall. The plan he proposed was shocking for his day, a bold innovation that bound all elements of the city together. According to this plan, the city would own the subway, finance construction, and charge rent, while a private backer would build and operate it, keeping the profits.

In the free-for-all that resulted from this daring proposition, the winner was John B. McDonald. He was a rough-and-ready Irish-American with thirty years of contracting under his belt. Despite his surly exterior, he had a genuine feeling for the men who worked under him that inspired their devotion and loyalty.

But McDonald needed to deposit a $7 million bond with the city comptroller, a large sum today but a staggering

ing amount then, in the days when a ten-hour shift meant no more than two dollars in your pocket. This seemed like an impossible barrier to surmount, but almost as if fate had been at work to bring the pieces of this intricate puzzle together, a savior materialized in

LEFT: John B. McDonald, circa 1904. NYTM

RIGHT: City Hall IRT station with advertising posters, circa 1920. NYTM

the person of August Belmont, the heir of an immense and newly minted fortune. He had something of his immigrant father's daring and imagination (the family name had originally been Schoenberg). But he also had the benefit of the very best American education and extremely powerful connections, having swaggered his way into New York's social elite with his thoroughbred horses and his patronage of the opera.

August Belmont, circa 1904. NYTM

Together the two became a dynamic team. And thus these two unlikely characters formed the company that was to be known as the Interborough Rapid Transit—the IRT.

Official ground-breaking ceremony for the IRT Rapid Transit Railroad on the steps of City Hall, March 24, 1900. NYTM

Opening ceremonies, City Hall, October 27, 1904. NYTM

In October 1904, on a brisk autumn day, the inauguration of the IRT took place. After four years of heroic labor, with all the world watching, one of the seven wonders of the modern world is complete. Officialdom struggles to find a way to mark the occasion with great pomp and circumstance. There are endless speeches, ribbon-cutting ceremonies, and an exclusive ceremonial ride for the "high hats" led by Mayor George McClellan, who runs the train from City Hall to 103rd Street with a silver operating handle made by Tiffany.

But the more meaningful celebration is to take place later that night, after all the officials and special guests go home. The doors are finally thrown open to the general public, the crowds of workers and immigrants whose lives will be profoundly altered by this event. There is wild cheering, singing, and dancing in the aisles; joyous crowds ride up and down in ecstasy all night. They epitomize the city's spontaneous response, which is to take possession of the subway as quickly as it can, to physically claim it, to make it its own. In the days that follow, some do this with delight, and others do it with complaints, but the simple fact is that the subway almost immediately becomes an underground mirror of New York, capturing its spirit, its speed, its vitality, its energy.

(2029) 50ᵀᴴ ST. STATION
7-14-1902

CHAPTER TWO

Miracles, Tragedies, and Fantastic Discoveries

A young man steps up to the witness stand in a hot, crowded courtroom in lower Manhattan. He is tall and thin, with dark, burning eyes; although at first glance he seems calm and self-possessed, there is a restlessness in him. As chief engineer for the Board of Rapid Transit Commissioners, he is assailed by questions from all sides.

After almost three hours of interrogation, he shows no signs of strain. In fact, he gives the impression that he is still waiting for the tough questions to come.

"The devil take him," one of the opposing lawyers is heard to mutter to another. "He's making fools of all of us." The courtroom is enthralled by this fierce young man; the most hardened skeptics are amazed by how much he knows.

"How can you remember all that?" a reporter asks him afterward.

"Engineers can't afford to make mistakes," he replies, turning away.

William Barclay Parsons had just turned thirty-five when August Belmont asked him to be chief engineer for

Breaking up pavement to begin construction of the 50th Street IRT station, July 1902. NYTM

William Barclay Parsons. NYTM

the Interborough Rapid Transit Company. Critics complained he was too young for the job; his own friends begged him to turn it down. But Parsons had been fascinated by the problem of urban mass transit ever since he had graduated from Columbia's School of Mines. His own ambition was at its peak: he wanted nothing less than to build a foundation for the city of New York.

"Do you think you have the maturity to see this plan through?" he was asked by one of the city elders toward the end of that day in court.

"Success doesn't depend on age," he answered without a moment's pause, "nor does it depend on will or enthusiasm. It depends on the rigorous analytical methods of a trained and educated mind." For Parsons, an engineer was one of the noblest things a man could be. Armed with reason, an engineer could alter the course of history. Although Parsons was possessed of tremendous will, he placed more stock in his own powers of analysis. He liked to quote Archimedes, the father of engineering: "Give me a lever and I'll move the world."

The next step for him was to draft and present a plan— and then to wait. And wait. The political infighting was endless, and though Parsons was a member of New York's elite, he could do nothing but wait. During this long period of inactivity, Parsons had to watch with frustration while other cities—Glasgow, Boston, Budapest—went forward with subways that New York so desperately needed.

William Barclay Parsons wields pickax: ground-breaking for work on IRT Subway begins at Bleecker and Greene Streets, Manhattan, March 1900. NYTM

"We have the worst transit problem in the world," he once said to a fellow engineer. "Are we to be the last to act?"

Unable to stand the suspense of waiting any longer, Parsons went to work on a surveying project in China, hoping against hope to be recalled. An entire year went by, and still no word from New York, and then one day a telegram arrived. All the opposition had finally been overcome; in great excitement, Parsons rushed back to Manhattan.

For the next four years, the building of the IRT consumed Parsons' days and nights. The design he had come up with was a masterpiece, though he had to struggle with almost insurmountable obstacles. For one thing, there was the dark-colored rock that formed Manhattan's base, a treacherous rock (Manhattan schist) flecked with sparkling mica chips that was almost impossible to cut through and yet vulnerable to decay.

Since the toughness of the rock made deep tunneling impractical, Parsons decided on a "cut-and-cover" method instead. This method required always keeping near the surface, never digging deep. He would cut through the pavement and dig out a trench that would ultimately become a tunnel when it was covered over again. The problem was that a maze of utilities lay directly underneath the surface of the streets, but Parsons wasn't fazed by this.

"Divert them," he said. "They can always be re-laid."

An elegant plan on paper, but its immediate results seemed like nothing short of a catastrophe. Dynamiting was constant, creating the sense of a city under siege: the sound of the blasts caused horses to rear up in terror, scattering pedestrians. The impact of the blasts produced showers of shattered glass, and a great many things toppled into the "subway hole," from street signs to building facades.

THIS HAS TO BE STOPPED! a headline proclaimed. LIFE IN NEW YORK IS NO LONGER CIVILIZED! "What Price for Progress?" a caption read under a Medusa's head of utility lines. Everyone became an expert overnight, claiming that Parsons had made a terrible mistake. But these were laymen, and Parsons, an engineer par excellence, had a total vision of what he was creating. Silent, proud, tenacious, he held to his plan.

But it wasn't only the explosions or the ripping apart of the streets that Parsons' critics complained about. It was the workers. An army of 7,700 men, they provided many occasions for genteel New York to cry SCANDAL! in the press. They came from all around the world, from Italy, Ireland, Sweden, South Africa. When plans for a two-mile tunnel were announced (it would run from Washington Heights to Fort George), miners poured in from all over the United States, as if it were another gold rush.

Many were from rural towns, and they were new to the ways of the city. When they came, they were educated fast, plunging into a lawless world of gambling, fighting, and whoring. There were endless complaints about the habits of these men, about their foul language, their violence, their uncivilized ways. And yet every one of them took enormous risks. And the pay was unbelievably low.

The miners who worked on the Washington Tunnel faced rock slides and being trapped in floods—for a day's wage of $3.75. And this was almost twice the amount the unskilled laborers received. The sandhogs (underwater diggers) were paid no more than $4.00 a day, toiling in compressed-air tunnels where the pressure could soar to 100 pounds per square inch. They were men of enormous strength, but the work they did took years out of their lives.

Over this ragged army of heroic, unruly men towered Parsons. He kept a close watch over the work they did, determined, inflexible, exacting, and severe.

Parsons' only reply to the cynics was to press forward with the work; his strongest rebuttal would lie in deeds, not words.

In all this struggle, there was only one incident that weakened his resolve. Parsons was inspecting the Murray Hill section of the tunnel with Major Ira A. Shaler, his appointed foreman and loyal friend. Shaler had stood by Parsons through thick and thin, never losing his conviction in the greatness of his plan.

Cut-and-cover construction on Broadway, south of Park Row. NYTM

"You don't have to be afraid with the General in charge," he would say to his crew when they were tired or discouraged. "If he says we can do it, then we can."

As they proceeded through the shaft, Parsons stopped dead in his tracks. He pointed his cane at a decayed-looking boulder a few feet ahead of them in the tunnel.

"That stone doesn't look right to me," he said to Shaler. "I'm afraid that we're going to have to turn back."

"With all due respect, General, the tunnel is perfectly safe," Shaler answered, stepping out from the wooden bracing fearlessly.

To Parsons' horror, the boulder came crashing down and Shaler was badly hurt. Parsons cried out for help, and workers immediately rushed in. When they finally got the injured man free, and were about to carry him out on a stretcher, he clutched at Parsons' arm.

"Come to the hospital with me, General," he managed to say. A few days later, Shaler died. After his funeral, Parsons walked into Belmont's office and told him that he wanted out.

"I've lost my best friend down there," he said to him. "I can't stomach this business anymore." But Belmont remained silent. He understood his chief engineer well enough to know he would never give up. He gave him time to mourn.

And of course he was right. Two weeks later, Parsons could be seen everywhere once again, giving orders, taking measurements, climbing down into the trenches with his men.

But while this was the tragedy that touched Parsons most personally, the greatest disaster occurred on October 24, 1903. It happened at the Fort George portal of the two-mile tunnel. The excavation was almost complete, and the foreman, an Irishman by the name of Timothy Sullivan, was anxious to get the work done. Sullivan had a reputation for being cautious and circumspect, but his unscrupulous contractor had been on his back, pushing him to work faster, to step up the pace, which meant extra dynamite blasts each day. On that October afternoon, a round of explosives was set off by Sullivan's crew. Although he usually waited two or three hours after an explosion before entering a tunnel, Sullivan waited only ten or fifteen minutes. As always, however, he worried about the safety of his crew, and so he went in alone to test the stability of the walls.

"Come ahead, boys!" Sullivan called out after what seemed like an eternity. No sooner had the workers reached the site than a 300-ton boulder came crashing down from the jagged roof of the tunnel. Drillers working near the entrance to the tunnel were literally knocked off their feet by a roaring blast of wind. The reverberations of the crash were felt for blocks around—and most of the men inside the tunnel died.

GRISLY DISASTER! the newspapers proclaimed. Rescuers worked for hours amid terrible screams and groans. A Roman Catholic priest by the name of Father Flynn stayed on the scene despite warnings that another crash might occur, scrambling up piles of blood-covered rock to deliver sacraments to the dying.

City Hall station, viewed from tracks at the south end, 1904. NYTM

Bleecker Street ceramic plaque, made by Grueby Faience Company, Boston, for Bleecker Street IRT station, 1904. NYTM

Times Square mosaic, Times Square IRT station, 1904. NYTM

Parsons agonized over the question of whether the speedup of the work was responsible for this tragedy. Once all the bodies had been freed from the merciless rock, Parsons came to the site to find out the truth. As he entered the tunnel, he thought he heard the soft murmur of water, and then he wondered whether he had only imagined it. But when he felt the moisture on the rocks and looked down at his fingers, he understood—it was a mixture of water and blood. The rock had been weakened by a hidden underground spring. There was a horizontal seam, a telltale sign, that had been concealed before the rock came apart. When he walked out of the tunnel, Parsons kept looking at the stains on his hands, making no effort to wipe them off. When a reporter asked him to make a comment, he looked at him as though he were a thousand miles away.

"The rock was weaker than any of us knew," he muttered, unable to say another word.

Apart from the tragedies, there were miracles—stories New Yorkers loved to marvel over. There was the tale of Marshall Mabey, who was working in a compressed-air tunnel when it collapsed like a punctured balloon. Mabey was sucked up through the bottom of the river but, astonishingly, he survived, providing an account that had the quality of a dream:

I closed my eyes and managed to get my hands over my head when I realized I was in sand and was being pushed by a tremendous force. I was being squeezed tighter than any girl ever held me and the pressure was all over me, especially on my head. . . . The last thing I recalled was seeing the Brooklyn Bridge above me while I was whirling around in the air.

During the digging of the subway, fantastic discoveries were made, like the prehistoric elephant (mastodon) bones unearthed at Dyckman Street. Dirt-covered diggers proudly held up the huge white bones while pedestrians flocked around, touching them in awe. There was the beautifully carved hull of an old Dutch ship that had gone down in the year 1613. The unearthing of Cat Alley brought back the flamboyant days of the so-called Rialto, a section of Houston Street where roving actors parodied passersby and gossiped about each other over sherry and cakes.

And in the midst of all these amazing things, these treasures that emerged from the city's depths, Parsons remained aloof, surveying the work with a scientific eye.

He knew that the fate of New York hung in the balance.

CHAPTER THREE

Growing Pains

*The long, tortuous evolution of New York's network
of subways is a story of countless entanglements;
perhaps no other issue of the period, certainly not
the tariff or free silver, bulked so large in New
York's consciousness, or was debated with more
heat and confusion.—Lately Thomas*

T he subway "puts on the ritz!" For the description of
a very special gathering in 1905—a tony society
get-together at the Belmont Hotel on Forty-second and
Park—we are indebted to AE, as he signs himself, one of
those fast-talking, charming interlopers who make a living by writing up the doings of the rich and famous for the
edification of the hoi polloi—make that "the man (and
woman) on the street." August Belmont is the gracious
host (a.k.a.: the Traction King. Though just what "traction"
royalty is, the society reporter neglects to explain). The
Vanderbilts and the Astors are there (of course), mingling
with the—well, the *you know who*s—dining on Cornish
game hens and venison in a regal salon as their host bides
his time, for he has asked them here to reveal his pride
and joy. At the height of the "elegant festivities," Belmont
springs his surprise. Will the honored guests do him the

New Utrecht Avenue station, Brooklyn; BRT Sea Beach line, June 1915. NYTM

favor of following him to the stairs? They all do, of course (he is not a man to refuse), and in a few moments the group is in a crowded bar in the subbasement of the hotel.

The party follows Belmont through the bar to a door which leads to Grand Central Station where the astonished guests find themselves making their way down a dimly lit flight of steps opening onto a deserted subway platform: what can Belmont be up to?

And then they see it: a carriage fit for a king, the *Mineola*, a fantasy in crimson and maroon (the Belmont colors), with velvet cushions, broadloom carpets, and paintings of mythological themes. The ceilings are pistachio green; touches of gold are reflected in panels of stained glass.

Belmont gives them a grand tour, showing them the gauges of polished brass that allow him to observe air pressure, current, voltage, and speed. And then there is the galley, with its electric oven and grill, and his rolltop desk, and his traveling library of leather-bound books.

It is a perfect fantasy train though it is an expensive one—the *Mineola* will cost more than the half million dollars allotted for the ornamentation of all forty-nine IRT stations—a fact which does not concern either Belmont or his guests, who sink into comfortable chairs and sip champagne as they speed toward the Belmont racetrack, with nothing but praise for their host.

TOP: The *Mineola*, circa 1904. Edward B. Watson Collection from the Shoreline Trolley Museum Library.

BOTTOM: The *Mineola*, interior with desk. NYTM

But if Belmont has his enthusiastic admirers, he has his detractors as well—and they are no less passionate. Among them is William Randolph Hearst, who constantly attacks Belmont in his newspapers, using both words and images—political cartoons, such as one depicting Belmont as a gigantic snake coiled around a subway car. The passengers are looking out the windows in alarm, some trying vainly to escape. The jaws of the snake gape wide; the caption reads: BELMONT IS NEVER SATISFIED.

But Belmont was used to attacks of all kinds. He often quoted his father's motto—"Let a man succeed and he'll pay for it"—and while he did not often condescend to answer his opponents, if he had wanted to, he could have silenced them by simply saying: "They couldn't have done it without me." That is, none of the banks wanted to take the risk of underwriting the new subway. They came to Belmont and said, "We need $50,000 to go along with the bid and we have to come up with it in an hour," and Belmont came up with the money and in *less* than an hour. What's more, Belmont never even bothered to read the contract and he never looked back. McDonald was desperate, and Belmont responded to his desperation on the principle that the subway was going to make New York City, surely an achievement he could point to with pride.

This heroic side to Belmont, however, Hearst was careful to hide from his readership. In the *New York American*, August Belmont was portrayed as a ruthless profiteer, enemy of the common man. There was bitter resentment when Belmont bought the Manhattan Railway in 1905, making its four elevated lines into a division of the IRT. And then this resentment turned to outrage when he took over the Metropolitan Street Railway in 1905, becoming the undisputed ruler of New York's street railways, elevated railways, *and* subways.

The Hearst papers charged Belmont with exploiting the needs of the poor—a charge the readership eagerly believed (his champagne parties in the *Mineola* did nothing to help dispel this impression). They argued that the subway should be controlled by the city. Still carrying the memory of Boss Tweed around with them, many New Yorkers couldn't forgive Belmont for profiting from the IRT—and it is true that the profits kept rolling in from 1904 until the end of World War I.

But the Hearst papers left out a crucial fact: the IRT under Belmont was a brilliant success, and it was constructed in an astonishingly short period of time. The heart of New York's subway system was built in a mere four years, and some of its most innovative features—twenty-four-hour service, express trains, uniform fares—were established at that time. Belmont understood the importance of hiring the very best men—and of keeping a close watch over them. "Every detail of every contract . . . was absolutely under Mr. Belmont's control," his secretary recalled as an old man, "and it was carried out one hundred percent honest."

Belmont was scrupulously honest, but still, he was a businessman, and he saw the subway with a businessman's eye. Overcrowding translated into profit in his mind, and the subway was overcrowded from the start. By 1908, it was carrying 800,000 riders a day, one-third above its maximum capacity. What did that endless flood of passengers mean? It meant policemen getting physical with passengers, prodding and poking at them as if they were so many cattle; it meant sexual molestation, pickpocketing, fainting, and fights; it meant daily exposure to incurable diseases like tuberculosis.

What was Belmont's response to overcrowding on this scale? Did he see it as a cry for expansion, for the addition of new lines?

In Belmont's view, congestion, particularly during rush hour, was no more objectionable than the convivial crush at the theater. "If a day ever comes when transportation during rush hours is done without crowding, *the Companies will fail financially*," he once wrote.

Apart from the tremendous costs of expansion (the projected cost of an expansion that would more than double the route mileage of the first two contracts was over $400 million, more than the cost of the Panama Canal), Belmont was afraid of losing the crowds, but his fears weren't founded in reality. Although he launched one of the greatest civic projects of his time, he wasn't able to recognize the subway crisis for what it was—the growing pains of twentieth-century New York.

■   ■   ■

Unlike Belmont, who rode the subway frequently, watching over its operation like a hawk, William Randolph Hearst didn't like going underground, nor did he like rubbing shoulders with the crowd. An introvert with an insatiable craving for drama, Hearst was in love with the invention of the car, making surprise appearances all over town and then roaring away in a cloud of dust. And yet, although the subway wasn't for him, he understood its value for the common man.

GIVE THE SUBWAYS TO THE PEOPLE! the Hearst papers cried. DOWN WITH THE CORRUPT BOSSES OF THE TRACTION TRUST! Heir to a gold fortune, Hearst had limited experience of the common man, but he was fiercely determined to be his champion. A big man with a high, almost feminine voice, Hearst used the newspapers as his megaphone. And he saw right away that the subway, which touched millions of lives, was a perfect theme for his populist press.

The issue would find itself cropping up in the most unlikely places. On a hot summer night in 1905, 12,000 New Yorkers turn out to attend a musical entertainment in Madison Square Garden. Among the crowd is a slender man with a neatly trimmed beard who doesn't usually go in for frivolous fare like this. But rumor has it that the musicale is going to be turned into a political rally, and George McAneny, a newspaper reporter turned reform politician, has come to see this media stunt with his own eyes.

The original cast of *Flora Dora* appears on the stage, clad in marvelous candy-cane pink walking costumes with black hats and lace parasols. They are still as stunning as when the show first hit Broadway, and they are greeted with whistles and applause.

And then all at once the audience grows still: William Randolph Hearst, mayoral candidate for the Municipal Ownership League, is entering his box. When the applause comes, it is long and thunderous; the original cast of *Flora Dora* is completely forgotten. The crowd breaks into political song, mocking Charles Murphy, the notorious boss of Tammany Hall. "Everybody woiks but

Moiphy," they sing over and over again. "He only rakes in the dough."

And now they begin chanting "Speech! Speech! Speech!" McAneny watches intently as Hearst rises to his feet. Hearst's voice is utterly transformed; he has mastered the art of the demagogue's roar. One by one, he drives home his favorite themes—municipal ownership of all public utilities, of the street railways, and, most importantly, of the subways.

McAneny listens to Hearst with a heavy heart, alarmed by the fervor of the crowd. What does Hearst know about the lives of the poor? What does he know about the real needs of New York?

McAneny fought hard for everything he achieved, growing up poor in Greenville, New Jersey, with little education. As a boy, he sold newspapers on the street, and by the time he was sixteen he made himself into a reporter, leaping at every story that came his way until he was getting assignments in Manhattan. He would later reminisce about how he struggled to find the right words, how he struggled to overcome his ignorance. The outcome of that struggle is a single-minded man who has now entered into the arena of politics, never forgetting the lessons of poverty, never ceasing to press for social reform.

"Hearst is a bad man for this city," would be McAneny's verdict that night, a judgment he repeated years later in an interview. Hearst dealt in half-truths; he never thought anything through. New subway lines were needed, Hearst had gotten that part right, but where would the money come from?

Hearst runs for mayor of New York in 1905, for governor in 1906, and for mayor again in 1909, filling the Manhattan sky with the most splendid fireworks the city has ever seen. Although he never succeeds in winning the race, his name becomes synonymous with the Triborough Plan. A PLAN TO SAVE NEW YORK! his papers proclaim. GOODBYE TO THE BELMONT MONOPOLY! All around the city, people are talking about the Triborough Plan; the newspapers—especially the *New York American*—cover the story in full detail.

Three major routes, the newspapers proclaimed, owned and operated by the city. A line connecting the Battery to 138th Street in the Bronx, with a branch extending to Forest Lawn Cemetery and Pelham Bay Park . . . a bridge loop that will go from Canal Street across the Williamsburg Bridge all through Brooklyn and back into Manhattan via the Manhattan Bridge . . . and last but not least, the Fourth Avenue line, linking the business district of Brooklyn to the outer reaches, all the way out to the shores of the Narrows!

The Triborough Plan is fashioned into the key to a utopian subway city, a city free of congestion, crime, and disease, and, above all, a city free of the Traction Trust.

But behind the scenes, a very different plan is slowly but surely taking shape. Instead of polarizing finance and government, it will bind them closely together; instead of pitting the IRT against a competitor, it will make it the nucleus of a vastly expanded system.

George McAneny, borough president of Manhattan as of 1910, is a key player in the development of this plan. But the fate of the subway will ultimately depend on the wisdom of William Gaynor, one of New York's most stubbornly independent mayors, a man who begins as a darling of Hearst's *New York American* and ends up in its gallery of villains.

Gaynor grew up on his father's farm in the town of Skeetersboro, near Utica, New York. Bookish and dreamy and given to talking to himself, he was almost useless when it came to doing chores. As a young man, he found his calling in the law, combining a keen analytical mind with a love of oratory. His speeches were full of quotations from *Don Quixote*, Marcus Aurelius, and Epictetus, and they were delivered with an air of defiance, as though he was challenging his countrymen to rise above what he once described as their suspicion of "literary fellers."

Gaynor identified with the man of limited means and feared the growing power of monopolies and trusts. "It isn't the lawyer that I see in court," he explained, "it's the litigant behind him, pale with anxiety and eating up his substance in dragged-out legal expenses. It is for his sake that I use all my authority to compel a more rapid determination of cases." As a Brooklyn judge, Gaynor was famous for his speed.

When he ran for mayor in 1909, New Yorkers had good reason to believe he would support the Triborough Plan. "Let me tell you," he went on record as saying, "if the city is going to build any more subways out of the money of the rent payers and taxpayers of this city, I want the city to own them absolutely, without a claim by anybody on earth." But when he was elected to office, he studied the subway question in depth and discovered that the Triborough Plan was seriously flawed.

"This plan is a disaster," Gaynor remarked to a colleague of his. "Has anyone considered the consequences? I'm all for giving the IRT a competitor, but not if it means a double-fare. Do you know what that would mean for the working man? As though his life isn't already hard enough!"

And when the new mayor reviewed the city budget and made a list of New York's most desperately needed improvements, he saw that the Triborough Plan would be ruinous, requiring an enormous initial outlay of money.

The future of the subway was up in the air, and everyone had his own theory about what should be done. Day after day, messengers delivered subway maps to Gaynor's office in City Hall, and night after night he pored over them, trying to find his way through a maze of hypothetical routes.

HOW MUCH LONGER MUST WE WAIT? the newspapers cried. But when it came to the subway, Gaynor took his time, turning a deaf ear to the shrill voices of his critics.

Theodore Shonts, president of the IRT, was one of the few people in New York who was happy about Gaynor's delay. The reason for this is that he was pushing an exciting new subway plan that would make the IRT into the heart of a unified system. It would be a system that could be built in a short time and that would connect every corner of the city, all under a single fare.

Convinced of the superiority of his plan and eager to see it realized, Shonts cast about for ways to make the mayor see the light. But how could Shonts convert Gaynor to his point of view? He hired a lawyer who happened to be the mayor's neighbor in Park Slope, a man by the name of Mirabeau Towns, but Towns' lobbying didn't produce any results.

So Shonts decided to take a leap of faith. The mayor had a weekend retreat, a sixty-acre farm called Deepwells on the north shore of Long Island. Here he could roam contentedly with his dogs and chat about crops and livestock with his neighbors and forget about the city. If one fact was known about Gaynor, it was that he hated to be disturbed while he was at Deepwells, but still, on a cold spring day in April 1910, Shonts drove out to Deepwells to pay the mayor a surprise visit—with Towns coming along to lend him moral support (at a fee of $5,000). When they got to the house, they waited for a while in the car, going over their strategy one more time—and suddenly realized they weren't alone. A figure in baggy pants and a thick woolen jacket was watching them closely from a nearby hill. As soon as the engine stopped, the figure leapt into motion, scrambling over a picket fence and disappearing from their sight. And now the two men were at a loss, since Gaynor was surely still outside, and if they knocked on the door there was every likelihood that a well-trained servant would turn them away. They were still trying to decide what they should do when the figure reappeared on the hill.

Ignoring Towns' cautious warnings, Shonts grabbed a bottle of champagne and headed toward the mayor alone. He was convinced, he said later, that before the day was out they would be drinking a toast to the new IRT.

For the next three hours, Towns sat shivering in the car while the sensibly dressed Gaynor and the thinly attired Shonts trudged up and down on the frozen ground. Gaynor never asked Shonts to come inside, although he offered him shots from the flask he was carrying in his pocket. By the end of the afternoon, Shonts was numb with cold, but he had gotten Gaynor to agree to review the financial records of the IRT.

After an extensive investigation, Gaynor concluded that the books of the IRT were absolutely clean. Gaynor's conversion was now complete: from this point on, he was "a rabid IRT man," in the words of George McAneny.

Some said Gaynor showed great courage in changing his position, but others said he had betrayed the city. Hearst was furious that Gaynor had turned against the Triborough Plan, and the two men became bitter enemies. The Hearst papers did everything in their power to bring the independent-minded Gaynor down. Gaynor fought back with all his might, defending himself with equal ferocity. Hearst's mind was "a howling wilderness," he said publicly, in the wake of a particularly savage attack.

"But what about your campaign promises?" Gaynor was often asked. "Haven't you deceived the people of New York?"

"Wise men change their minds; fools don't," was Gaynor's reply.

It took two more years before a solution to the subway crisis was found, and the path was terribly intricate. Gaynor formed a committee to oversee the search, but when he asked one of its members to head the committee, he staunchly refused, as a way of protesting the abandonment of the Triborough. When he turned to the second man, he did the same. Gaynor turned to the third man wearily, fixing him with his probing gaze.

"I'm afraid these gentlemen don't want to serve," he said. "Will you take it, Mr. McAneny?"

At that same moment, a whiskered gentleman, Colonel Timothy S. Williams, president of the Brooklyn Rapid Transit, was waiting outside McAneny's office at City Hall. McAneny didn't come back from his meeting until the end of the day, but the gentleman waited patiently, holding a huge roll of maps on his knees. When McAneny finally returned, he was surprised to find the stranger waiting for him.

Postcard, "Tunnel Under the New York East River," circa 1908. NYTM

Handing McAneny the roll of maps, he introduced himself and followed him into his office as he explained his goal: dividing the lines between the IRT and the BRT in a way that would avoid repetition.

The Dual Contract System was conceived that day, although it would be months before the scheme was fully developed. McAneny remembered Colonel Williams as "a quiet little gentleman," but the plan he put forward was enormously ambitious. The IRT and the BRT would be joined into an interlocking pair, with the IRT expanding into the Bronx and the BRT expanding into new regions of Brooklyn. Track mileage would be tripled and subway mileage would be greatly expanded, forever altering the shape of the city.

These changes were achieved only after months and months of negotiation in the Tribute Building at 154

Nassau Street. Representatives of the IRT and the BRT faced each other across an old oaken table, and the city's representatives were grouped around the table as well. The bargaining that went on over the old table was fierce, with each party trying to corner the best deal. After one particularly heated session, Shonts emerged, looking wild-eyed and disheveled.

"I was fairly well-dressed when I went into that room," he said to a reporter waiting in the hall, "but they've taken away everything but my shirt, and they would have taken that too, if we hadn't adjourned."

What went on at 154 Nassau Street? Nothing short of a treaty between two mighty subway nations, a treaty that would involve amending the constitution of New York, passing new laws, and putting the Triborough proposal to rest.

After six months of bargaining, an agreement was reached, a very short time given the complexity of the deal. The contracts were finally approved on March 19, 1913, filling a book that was six inches thick. The city of New York was to contribute the lion's share—$164 million, chiefly for underground subway construction. The IRT and the BRT were to put up $77 million and $61 million, respectively.

"Mark my words—the Dual Subway System will be the greatest industrial feat of this age," Gaynor remarked.

Gaynor never lived to see his prediction come true, dying shortly after his term was over, but for the people of New York his name was forever linked to it. When Gaynor died, his body was laid to rest in the rotunda at City Hall. The first citizen who came to pay his respects was a crippled bootblack who worked the Staten Island Ferry. Thousands of other New Yorkers followed him; when the doors closed, 20,000 had to be turned away. The next day, tens of thousands lined the streets, from City Hall to Greenwood Cemetery in Brooklyn.

"He was the people's mayor," one man said. "You could always count on him to fight for us."

And his greatest victory on the people's behalf was the Dual Subway System.

Malbone Street wreck, 1918. Worker standing on the remains of BRT el car inside the Malbone Street tunnel. Collection of Donald W. Harold

CHAPTER FOUR

The Subway Comes of Age

I magine that you are very young, and that you are standing in a long, long line, eagerly waiting for a signal that never seems to come. You and your class-mates—in fact, every student in your school—have been anticipating this day for weeks. "A great honor has been granted to us," your teachers have been saying. "One day you'll tell your children about this historic ride. . . ." And what's more, Coney Island is at the end of that magical ride—a place you've only heard about—and as you try to picture the wonders of Steeple-Chase Park and the ocean, a force catches you up and hurls you forward, sweeping you down into the station at Chambers Street.

"Look at the cars!" you hear an older boy cry. You try to catch a glimpse of the train before you are pushed on board. The cars are different from any you've ever seen before: they are the color of dark chocolate, with shiny black roofs, and they are bigger than the old maroon trains that have been around ever since you were born.

The next thing you know, you are hurtling through the tunnel, and then all at once you emerge into dazzling light, shooting across the one-and-a-half-mile stretch of water that has always made Brooklyn seem so far away. In less than an hour, you'll arrive at Coney Island, pleasure land. "One nickel will get you there." A nickel miracle.

On June 22, 1915, the first subway line of the BRT was opened to the general public. By a special dispensation of Colonel Williams, president of the BRT, 1,100 school-children were invited to become the first riders of the new Brooklyn line. Brooklyn had been slow to enter subway history, but when it did, it entered in style. Its new all-steel cars, which were still in use in the 1970s, made the composite cars of the IRT—steel structures and frames, with wooden sides—look out of date. A variety of seating was available for the first time, instead of two rows of seats facing each other. The seats themselves were tested on one hundred men and women of various racial descrip-tion, earning the praise of the American Posture League, which declared them to be compatible with the natural contours of the human body.

June 22 was also an important day in the history of Queens. The Steinway Tunnel, which had been completed for trolley use in 1907 only to be abandoned because of a franchise dispute until 1913, was finally opened for sub-way use, linking Manhattan to Queens.

STEINWAY-QUEENS TUNNEL OPENS AT LAST

read a typical real estate ad in the *New York Times* of June 1915.

SEVERAL LOTS ADJOINING SITE FOR NEW POST OFFICE BUILDING IN LONG ISLAND CITY RECENTLY PURCHASED BY THE UNITED STATES GOVERNMENT FOR SALE AT BIG BARGAIN PRICE

With the opening of the Fourth Avenue line of the BRT and the Steinway-Queens Tunnel, the Dual System was officially launched. By the time the Dual System was complete, the

BRT controlled 271 route miles of the city's total of 629.7, and what we know today as the BMT was essentially in place, with the exception of the Dyre Avenue line. Brooklyn and Queens were intricately connected to Manhattan and the Bronx, and land was being developed at a furious pace.

The Dual System, in the words of Clifton Hood, opened up "a vast crescent of undeveloped land that stretched from the North Bronx, across Queens, and through Brooklyn." That land—woods, meadows, farm-lands, rolling hills—was swallowed up by housing. And now the dream of the Progressives finally came true: the old tenement districts of Manhattan began to empty out. Ninety percent of the population growth of New York between 1910 and 1940 occurred in the so-called subway suburbs of Manhattan. During the same period of time, the population of the Lower East Side, to take just one example, fell by 60 percent.

Immigrants who had lived without the most basic amenities now began flocking to new-law tenements, named after a 1901 municipal reform that established new standards for low-income housing. "We didn't call them tenements," an Italian mason said, "we called them apart-ment houses, because that's what they really were. To us, a tenement was a dump." Bathrooms instead of outhouses, separate kitchens, hot running water, and, most impor-tantly of all, air and light, not to mention modern conven-iences that seemed out of this world—automated elevators, mail chutes, garbage disposal. Middle-class comforts were suddenly available to the working class at the same rents they had paid in the slums. For the immi-grants who had risked everything only to land in Green-wich Village, the Lower East Side, or the notorious Five Points, it must have seemed as though fortune's wheel had finally turned in their favor. An Italian immigrant rejoiced over the space to plant a garden, a Jewish immi-grant wept over finally having privacy—the unrestrained joy of a whole generation of immigrants was recalled vividly even decades later.

Tides of immigrants kept sweeping into New York, but instead of being concentrated in lower Manhattan, they were pouring into Brooklyn, Queens, and the Bronx. Jewish, Irish, Italian, German, Polish, Russian, and Greek, they formed intimate cells in ever-multiplying neighborhoods within which older ways of life were intricately encoded. By 1930, the Bronx was the sixth largest city in the country, with a population of over one million. Between 1910 and 1940, the population of Queens rose by 218 percent, and the population of Brooklyn rose by 165 percent. By 1930, Brooklyn overtook Manhattan as the most heavily populated of all the five boroughs.

And while neighborhood after neighborhood was springing up along the new lines of the Dual System, the work of construction was pressing forward underground. The era of the subway hole gave way to the era of decked roadway construction; wherever possible, huge timbers were positioned under wooden decking and kept in place until the steel skeleton of the subway had been erected, a technique that was far less disruptive to the life of the city. Because poisonous gases easily got trapped in the confined space between the decking and the street, service pipes had to be carefully rerouted with bypass pipes laid close to the street's surface or supported on trestles above the sidewalks.

Between the rocky north and the sandy south, a variety of different land conditions prevailed, calling for a variety of innovative construction techniques. And new river crossings, eight in all, called for the perfecting of tunneling methods that were still quite new. Twenty thousand men labored and toiled in a project that resulted in the greatest subway system in the world. Thanks to the guiding presence of some two thousand engineers, there were fewer accidents than there had been previously, although cave-ins and tunnel explosions were still reported in the newspapers.

But the worst accident took place in 1918, just three years after the opening of the BRT, and construction methods had nothing to do with it.

During the summer of 1918, the BRT fired some forty of its motormen (roughly 10 percent). The reason given for the firings? Failure to comply with the regulations of the BRT. But an outside review found that twenty-nine of these men had broken only one unwritten rule: they had dared to show their faces at union meetings, an action that was enough to brand them as Communists in the second decade of the twentieth century.

The firings were contested by the Brotherhood of Locomotive Engineers, and the BRT eventually agreed to hire back the men, but it refused to recognize the union, pushing the company union instead. The Brotherhood was infuriated by this, and on November 1, at 5:00 A.M., a group of motormen and train guards walked off their jobs.

And so it was that a man who went by the name of Billy Lewis was asked to operate a rush-hour train on the Brighton Beach line. He wasn't a motorman, he was a crew dispatcher, and his real name wasn't Lewis, it was Luciano. Dark and slender, he was no more than twenty-five years old, and he was struggling to make his way in the world. The assignment represented an incredible break for him, but it came to him at the wrong time. He was still recovering from the Spanish influenza, an illness that had claimed his three-year-old daughter's life only a few days before. (When the day was over, he would be a survivor once again, and his burden of guilt would be even harder to bear.)

Before November 1, Luciano was many steps away from being a motorman, the top of the ladder in terms of status and pay. So far his work had consisted of recording the comings and goings of personnel, a job that was a notch above being a conductor, and yet, because it was essentially office work, infinitely more tedious. The two and a half hours of classroom training that Luciano had received were not enough to prepare him for the challenge that was suddenly tossed his way. Those two and a half hours were designed to prepare him for the job of motor switchman. His training as a motorman was confined to

Malbone Street wreck, 1918. BRT el car at 36th Street Yard after the disaster. Collection of Donald W. Harold

two days of riding in the cab with motormen in anticipation of the strike, as opposed to the sixty hours of instruction usually required.

Luciano had started work at 5:00 A.M. in his usual capacity as a crew dispatcher. With the strike on, it was an exhausting day: everyone was scrambling to find men to fill in the gaps. At 4:30, Luciano was ready to go home, but there was one last problem that remained to be solved. The rush hour had been covered, with the exception of one twenty-mile run, a trip from Kings Highway to Manhattan via the Brooklyn Bridge and then back to Brighton Beach, with an ordinary running time of one hour and forty minutes.

One of the mysteries of what happened on Malbone Street remains unsolved to this day. Why did Luciano agree to operate a rush-hour train on a dark November night on a route he was unfamiliar with? Did he fear for his job? Was he blinded by ambition? Did he allow himself to be pressured into it? Or did he have the fatalistic courage that sometimes comes with grief, the sense that the worst has already come to pass?

"A man has to make a living," Luciano said to a reporter who asked him what went through his mind that night. Only a few days before, he had lost his second child—four years earlier, another daughter had died.

Luciano set out from the Kings Highway Yard at 5:15 P.M., completely alone in the cab of the train. In the course of his journey, he pulled into the Thirty-sixth Street station on the Fifth Avenue line, only a block away from his house on Thirty-fourth. Just one block away, his wife was waiting for him.

The train crossed the Brooklyn Bridge into Manhattan without incident, picking up passengers at Park Row.

When he discovered that his marker lights weren't working, Luciano hung out a white lantern to let the switch operator know. Crossing Brooklyn Bridge back to Brooklyn, he kept the train under control, successfully maneuvering a steep downhill grade, steeper than the grade between Crown Heights and Prospect Park, where he was to lose control of the train. At Franklin Avenue, the train was switched onto the Fulton Street line, even though its destination was Brighton Beach. Following BRT procedures, Luciano got out of the train, conferred with the switch operator, backed up the train, and rerouted it to the Brighton Beach line, an operation that resulted in a delay of eight minutes.

Leaving Park Place for Prospect Park, Luciano went down an 1,800-foot downhill grade without using the brakes to check the train's gathering speed. The tunnel had been put into service only a few weeks before, and Luciano didn't know there was a sharp S-shaped curve directly in front of it. Hitting that fatal curve, the first car was derailed, and then the second car veered off the tracks. The next two cars stayed on the tracks, but the middle cars smashed into the new tunnel walls. The roof and sides of one car were torn away; the next car was utterly destroyed. Ninety-three passengers died in the course of that night, most of them victims of massive head injuries.

After the crash, Luciano stumbled out of the cab, walking through the cars in a state of shock. He was still gripping the brake and motor handles, and he seemed to be walking in his sleep, unable to react to the horror all around him. An attorney sitting in the first car of the train, directly behind the motorman's cab, called out to him.

"What happened?"

Luciano's reply was simple enough: "I lost control."

Staggering off the train, Luciano finally made his way home. Accounts differ as to what happened later that night: some say the police came to take Luciano away, and others say he turned himself in.

Medical workers, foremen, and clergymen worked all through the night in the hellish tunnel. An emergency station was set up in Ebbet's Field, and the Kings County Morgue was overflowing with the dead.

The words "Malbone Street" became so imbued with tragedy that the street was renamed Empire Boulevard. Though if you go to Brooklyn, you'll find a little section of street that still goes by the name of *Malbone*, a fragment that no one bothered to ritually cover.

Colonel Williams, president of the BRT, who had been instrumental in the planning of the Dual Contracts, resigned in the wake of Malbone Street, retiring to Long Island. He had seen a glorious new subway system appear in Brooklyn, and he had lived through its darkest hour.

On December 31, 1918, the BRT went into receivership, an event often associated with the Malbone Street disaster but actually caused by financial problems that had been dogging it from the start.

On November 1, peace treaties were being deliberated in Europe, and the first day of peace was observed. The day began on a note of celebration, but it ended in horror and grief. In the days and weeks afterward, the city followed the trial of Luciano, who was eventually acquitted of manslaughter. The subway carried its own burden of sorrow now—but subway ridership held steady, and life went on.

CHAPTER FIVE

Nickel and Skyscraper

F ebruary 17, 1919. A group of black soldiers gets onto a downtown train, carrying trumpets, saxophones, and horns. Their uniforms are clean and freshly pressed, but their instruments are as scratched and dented as their tin hats. As the train pulls out of the station, one of the soldiers begins to play "All of No Man's Land Is Ours," and within seconds the car is flooded with the sound of jazz. Wherever the train stops, new passengers try to squeeze in, joining the crush. When the soldiers pile out and head for the 71st Regiment Armory on Fourth Avenue (now Park Avenue South) at Thirty-first, where a celebration is being held in their honor, a mob of fans runs after them.

The men belong to the 369th U.S. Infantry, also known as the Harlem Hellfighters. An all-black infantry, they have become legendary in France, taking the spirit of jazz everywhere, from hospital beds to the battlefield.

All through the war, they have been admired by the French, who have awarded them the French Croix de Guerre, an honor no other American infantry unit has ever received. "The French gave us the Croix de Guerre," one of their songs goes, lamenting American racism, "and the U.S. Army gave us the Double Cross."

IRT LV (low voltage) motor car, circa 1930. NYTM

But this day is different. Half a million New Yorkers have turned out to welcome them home as they march up Fifth Avenue, with another half million waiting for them in Harlem. Until they reach Harlem, they march in tight, French-style formation to the tune of traditional French marches, but as soon as they turn the corner onto Lenox Avenue, the band breaks into "Here Comes My Daddy Now!" and the crowd rushes forward ecstatically.

The Harlem that is home to the 369th U.S. Infantry hadn't existed twenty years earlier. As soon as the route of the first subway line was revealed, real estate developers went into a building frenzy. Middle-class housing went up all over Harlem—but middle-class New Yorkers were maddeningly slow to respond. And then an African-American realtor by the name of Philip Paton bought up as many buildings as he could, urging black tenants to leave the slums of the Lower West Side.

By 1913, three quarters of all the blacks in New York had made the move uptown. In an astonishingly short period of time, Harlem became what the Reverend Adam Clayton Powell Sr. described as "a symbol of liberty and the Promised Land to Negroes everywhere." "If my race can make Harlem," one man said, "good Lord, what *can't* it do?"

During the 1920s, Harlem enjoyed its Renaissance, and what F. Scott Fitzgerald called the Jazz Age suddenly took off. But before the boom years of the Roaring Twenties, no one seemed to have enough money.

Whether they lived in Harlem, Brooklyn, Queens, or the Bronx, American soldiers returning from the Great War found themselves up against the same hard facts: the cost of living ran very high, and it was tougher than ever to find a job. 100,000 NEW YORKERS RECEIVE EVICTION NOTICES IN 1919! a newspaper headline proclaimed. "First you're a hero and then you're a bum," one soldier complained, nursing a tumbler of bootleg whiskey.

In the years of postwar inflation, when the prices of consumer goods went up a dizzying 56 percent, the cost of a subway ride was still just a nickel. The nickel fare was a balm to the ridership, but it did lasting damage to the companies. The cost of building a subway car was twice what it had been in 1914, when the Dual Contracts were signed. Steel was hard to come by and the cost of labor had gone up—but the subway fare remained the same. Cost-cutting measures were introduced everywhere, lowering the standards August Belmont had prided himself on.

"I saw a car with clean windows today," Frank Hedley, president of the IRT, told a group of employees. "When I got back to the office I raised hell to find out who cleaned all those windows and spent all that money."

Nickel fare. NYTM

Dirty, dilapidated, poorly maintained, the subway became a source of endless complaints, but shabby as it was, it continued to work its magic, conjuring up cities within cities. A tidal wave of workers broke over midtown Manhattan every morning, rushing back to the outer boroughs at the end of the day. When night fell, a new wave of riders surfaced on the streets, flocking to the silver screen. Motion picture palaces were proliferating on Times Square, and you could get there for a nickel. The working class rode the subway as never before, forging the labyrinth of the city.

Postwar inflation temporarily concealed the fact that the Great War had done wonders for New York. Coming out way ahead of its debts, Manhattan became the nerve center of a second industrial revolution. For the first time in history, consumer goods were being produced and packaged for the masses. Drawing on its vast reserves of skill and ambition, New York took a leading role in creating the modern consumer. The workforce that gathered in the skyscrapers of Manhattan was one of the most dynamic the world had ever seen. Without the subway, this concentration of talent could never have been achieved— and yet the subway itself was in terrible trouble.

Before World War I, the subway was a thriving enterprise; after the war, it plunged into a downward spiral. By 1918, the BRT had gone into receivership, and the IRT was to suffer the same fate in 1932.

Everyone knew the subway needed more money, but no one wanted it to come out of their own pockets. A subway nickel became a powerful thing: it could make or break a political career. "Look what happened in 1906," politicians whispered among themselves, recalling the mayhem that ensued when the (presubway) BRT imposed a ten-cent fare on the Coney Island el.

The place, a courtroom in downtown Brooklyn; the presiding judge is the Honorable William Gaynor. He has listened to the arguments on both sides, nodding

impatiently from time to time. "Raising the fare would set a dangerous precedent," he finally tells the court. "We would be foolish to open this Pandora's box. Despite the unusual length of its run, the fare on the Coney Island El will continue to be a nickel."

Ignoring the ruling, the BRT hires 250 trained "inspectors" to collect the extra five cents. In the days that follow, 1,000 rebellious passengers are thrown off the els, including an entire car, which is uncoupled from a train and abandoned. The passengers retaliate by vandalizing the car, using parts of it to build a bonfire. When their party ends, the sun is coming up, and the roof of the car is completely demolished.

The inspectors become increasingly brutal, coming down hard on the troublemakers. When the borough president of Brooklyn refuses to pay the ten-cent fare, he is kicked off the train like everyone else. "You'll regret this," he shouts helplessly, shaking his fist at the departing train. By that evening, several Brooklyn jails are filled with BRT employees.

In the midst of all these skirmishes, the naked body of an adolescent girl is found at the bottom of Coney Island Creek. Many Brooklynites are convinced she was the victim of one of the company thugs, and the BRT is covered with scandal.

If nonbelievers kept their views to themselves, supporters of the five-cent fare tended to be passionate. Politicians gained tremendous mileage from this cause, riding on a crest of public enthusiasm. John B. Hylan would never have become mayor if he hadn't fought hard for the subway nickel. "The five-cent fare is the cornerstone of that edifice that we call New York," Hylan proclaimed, a genuinely held conviction that endeared him to Hearst, producing one of the oddest couplings in transit history.

John Hylan was a man without a past when he entered the world of New York politics. He had been a judge in

Brooklyn, but unlike the poker-faced William Gaynor, he hadn't made a name for himself there. When he put in his bid for mayor of New York, the newspapers weren't kind to him. The *New York Times* described him as a man of "marvelous mental density," and he was often represented as a bungling comedian. But he was fiercely committed to the municipal subway and the five-cent fare, and as a result the *New York American* was on his side.

"Who is Hylan?" was the question of the hour. The answer that began to circulate read like a page from Horatio Alger.

Hylan was the farm boy who makes good in the big city, soaring above his humble beginnings. He came to Brooklyn with a dream in his heart and $2.50 in his pockets. He was a good man, an honest man, the salt of the earth, and he never forgot what it meant to be poor. As a politician, he was a champion of the people, a true democrat.

What was John Hylan really like? Quick to act, slow to forgive; driven by ambition, hobbled by resentment. Hylan grew up poor on a struggling farm in Greene County, New York, and he was very eager to get out. At an early age, he took to railroading, leaving his family behind. Working different jobs, he eventually made his way to Brooklyn, where he was employed by the Kings County Elevated Railroad, a subsidiary of the BRT. Rising easily through the ranks, he became an engineer by the

BMT Standards in a yard, circa 1924. NYTM

time he was twenty-three years old. And then he got married and his sense of himself changed: all at once he decided he wanted a career in law. Driving an engine at night, he attended classes during the day, and he pursued a clerkship at a Long Island City law firm at the same time. On a cold winter night in 1897, the strain of this life finally got the better of him.

As he guided his steam-powered el around the curve at Navy Street, the young Hylan was preoccupied. His bar examinations were coming up and, as he mentioned years later in his autobiography, he was busily preparing for them. As he struggled with a difficult case in the law, his mind flashed onto his father's farm. How depressing and limited life was there. And then all at once he saw a figure walking along the tracks, a stooped old man in overalls. Paralyzed for an instant, he finally managed to throw on the brakes, barely avoiding an accident.

Hylan got off the train, his heart pounding dully in his chest. What was an old man doing on the tracks? When he realized with horror that it was Barton, his supervisor, he felt sick to his stomach.

Hylan was charged with driving his train too fast and summarily stripped of his job. But he was always convinced that the charges were false, and that the truth was that he had saved Barton's life. "Had I been moving fast, nothing would have saved him," Hylan insisted in his autobiography. It was Barton who was negligent, Hylan maintained, but the BRT needed a scapegoat and so they fired him.

Hylan's rage against the BRT was a burning ember that never grew cold. Twenty-one years later, it was fanned into flame by the news of the Malbone Street wreck.

Invoking an obscure law he remembered from his student days, Hylan appointed himself "committing magistrate" of an investigation into the causes of the accident.

"The hearings were run like a carnival," one observer recalled. "No one seemed to care about due process or rules of order." Luciano found a sympathetic audience in the mayor, but Hylan played the part of hanging judge in the case against the BRT. And yet, if it hadn't been for the nickel fare, the Malbone Street wreck might never have happened. After all, the nickel fare was costing the companies dearly. And it was the transit workers who ended up paying the price, in the form of layoffs and salary cuts. Men like Luciano were part of a vicious cycle—but Hylan still stood staunchly by the subway nickel.

Years go by, and on an August afternoon in the year 1922, as the city reels from the summer heat, reporters hurry up the steps of City Hall to attend a briefing on Mayor Hylan's new subway plan. Hylan's secretary, who happens to be his son-in-law, unfurls a large subway map.

"The mayor has asked me to convey his regrets at not being able to be here today," he begins.

"I wish I couldn't be here," one reporter calls out to laughter (a remark that makes the rounds, since everyone knows that the mayor is at the Saratoga Springs racetrack, along with his friend Hearst and the rest of fashionable New York).

"The municipal subway will bring desperately needed lines to the built-up districts of New York," Hylan's secretary reads from a prepared text. "It will also recapture two important lines from the BRT and the IRT, the Fourth Avenue line in Brooklyn and the West Side line in Manhattan."

The sweating reporters scribble away eagerly, getting down everything they need. By that night, the newspapers are carrying the latest subway story.

THE INDEPENDENT SUBWAY SENDS A RIPPLE OF FEAR THROUGH THE TRACTION TRUST!
674 million dollars to build! . . . but the way things go, it will probably be more.

The papers are filled with disbelief and criticism. What do they mean by "recapturing"? Is this just a fancy way of saying that the city is going to take over two major routes? And even more to the point, where is the money going to come from?

Before the plan can be acted on, it has to meet with the approval of the Transit Commission. George McAneny, head of the Transit Commission, has serious problems with Hylan's scheme. The so-called recapturing of lines is a sticking point: the routes in question can't be given up without destroying the integrity of his brainchild, the Dual System.

Hylan mounts an all-out media campaign on behalf of the Independent Subway. He makes public appeals via the radio—these are the early days of WNYC—and the Hearst papers champion his cause. But then one day he goes too far, and ends up paying an enormous price.

In the summer of 1924, two BRT trains collide near the Ocean Parkway station of the Brighton Beach line, killing one passenger and injuring thirty. Hylan seizes this occasion to mount a frontal attack on the Transit Commission. Appealing to Alfred E. Smith, the brilliant governor of New York, he demands the removal of McAneny, Leroy T. Harkness, and John F. O'Ryan, charging them with "willful neglect of and failure to discharge duty, misconduct and inefficiency."

Governor Smith sabotages Hylan's move by calling for a general transit investigation in order to determine whether there is sufficient justification for a trial. Smith fully intends for the investigation to turn on Hylan; although Hylan doesn't know it, the governor has lost confidence in him. (Years later, Smith writes that he had come to believe that Hylan had fallen under the spell of Hearst and that Hylan's reelection "would give Hearst too great an influence in the government of New York." Smith has his own reasons for hating Hearst, but that's another story.)

The investigation brings to light the perversity of Hylan's subway policies. In his zeal to thwart the power of

IND R-4 "A" Train at 207th Street station, 1932. NYTM

the older companies, Hylan has contributed to New York's subway crisis. Again and again, he has stood in the way of the subway construction approved by the Dual Contracts. He has prevented the completion of the Canarsie and Nassau Street line; he has blocked the improvement of shops and yards for repair; he has even obstructed the acquisition of new cars.

Testimony is heard in December of 1924 and in January of 1925. A few months later, Hylan suffers a crushing defeat in the 1925 mayoral campaign. James Walker, Al Smith's candidate, slides into Hylan's place. "Gentleman Jimmy" has an excellent subway record—as a state senator, he has always defended the five-cent fare, and he has backed legislation that enables Hylan to move on the municipal subway.

A few months before he is defeated by Walker, Hylan plunges a silver-plated shovel into a plot of ground at the intersection of St. Nicholas Avenue and West 123rd. Two thousand New Yorkers gather at Hancock Square in Washington Heights to witness this groundbreaking ceremony. In his speech to them, Hylan is visibly moved, assuming an almost prophetic stance. With tears in his eyes, he looks forward to "the emancipation of the people of the city of New York from the serfdom imposed by the most powerful dictatorship ever encountered" in its history. The Traction Trust is conjured up in all its greed and infamy, and Hylan crushes it once again.

On September 10, 1932, the Eighth Avenue line—the first installment of the IND—went into service. The dream of a municipal subway had finally come true, and yet there was no ceremony to mark this historic event. At 12:01 P.M., all the stations opened their gates and the crowds rushed blindly down the steps, unaware of the bitter struggles that had made this moment possible.

A latecomer in the transit history of New York, the IND was a very different creature from its forebears. The older companies were pioneers, forging paths to underpopulated areas of New York; the IND, which had no subsidy, couldn't afford to venture into the unknown. This was the metropolitan subway as opposed to the subway as an engine of urban expansion. Confined to already builtup areas, the IND redefined the subway's historic role, a change that Clifton Hood has described as a "critical concession" to the automobile.

The building of the IND was a gargantuan enterprise. Constructed piecemeal during the Great Depression, it took seven million man-hours to complete. Penetrating the most highly developed districts of New York, construction was never simple or straightforward. By the time it was finished in 1940, 26 miles of water and gas pipes,

350 miles of electrical conduits, and 18 miles of sewers had been rerouted.

By the time the Eighth Avenue line opened in 1932, what F. Scott Fitzgerald described as the "steady golden roar" of the twenties had died down forever. For one giddy decade, New York had entertained the dream that every man could be rich. At the height of this fever, shoeshine boys were sharing trading tips with businessmen. One skyscraper had soared up after another, great speculative towers built on the subway's back—and then the surge of speculation came to an end, leaving a trail of shattered fortunes in its wake.

Built between 1930 and 1931, the Empire State Building rose up in an astonishingly short period of fourteen months, defying the new force of gravity that was dragging at the city. The Empire State Building, like the IND, was at once a triumph and a boondoggle. It wasn't until 1950 that it became profitable—and similarly, the IND was financially troubled from the start. Conceived as a weapon against the older lines, it didn't operate in tandem with them, running up huge deficits. Divided into short stretches, each with a separate contract, it involved a great deal of patronage.

"The city didn't get what it paid for," a financial expert quipped, "although it certainly paid for what it got."

Despite these problems, the IND brought fifty-nine desperately needed route miles to the New York subway. City-owned and city-run, it paved the way for unification.

CHAPTER SIX

From the Great Depression to the World's Fair

S ubways are built with pickaxes, not thoraxes," Mayor Walker liked to say, washing his hands of subway politics. "Walker Says it with Shovels," a pamphlet proclaimed. "City Uses Shovels to Tell Subway Policy."

But no matter what he told the people of New York, subway dealings during the Walker years were anything but simple and direct.

A hot summer night. Central Park. A spray of silver is shooting up into the sky; it is the fountain on the rooftop of the Casino.

"Will you still love me in December as you do in May?" a tenor sings, and then the orchestra picks up the theme. (Jimmy Walker wrote this song in his vaudeville days, and in the world of the Casino it is his theme song, his leitmotif.)

A superb dancer, the mayor takes to the floor with a beautiful girl in a clinging gown. "Will you still love me?" he

The dismantling of the Sixth Avenue El and the building of the Sixth Avenue subway, circa 1939. NYTM

whispers in her ear, as though he is afraid she will slip away. Although he is facing a corruption investigation the next day, Walker is in excellent form. Here in the Black and Gold Room, spirits are running high; champagne passes from the trunks of limousines to the crystal glasses raised by intoxicated guests.

Walker's upstairs office, a deep, secluded chamber with a heavy sound-proofed door, remains unused all night long, as though Walker is determined to show that he doesn't need time to prepare. On most nights, the mayor holds court beneath a marvelous ceiling of gold leaf while envelopes of money pass back and forth—including envelopes from subway contractors.

At around three in the morning, one of Walker's cronies whispers to him that he'd better get home and get some beauty sleep. When he appears on the steps of the county courthouse in Foley Square the next day, he looks "too good for a politician," as a reporter writes of him, slim and elegant in a finely tailored suit. Five thousand admirers turn out to cheer him on; Gentleman Jimmy, with all his faults, is greatly beloved. But although he handles himself with his usual aplomb, the investigation drags on and on, and it gradually emerges that he has pocketed a staggering $1 million in kickbacks, payments he shrugs off as beneficences.

For some people, the subway meant patronage; for others, it was a source of honest work. During the Depression, finding a steady job was nothing short of a miracle, and the subway threw out lifelines to thousands of men, even as it was struggling to stay afloat.

Take one of the thousands of stories that were recorded so that future generations would understand what life in New York was like in those days. He was a hardworking Irishman who suddenly found himself with nowhere to turn. He had lost his job at the beginning of the year, and all his attempts to find work since then had failed. Evicted in March, he had been staying at his mother-in-law's with his wife and two daughters, but now she wanted them out.

Years later, he told an interviewer how he had spent that night walking the streets in despair, passing the vast settlement of ragged hovels in Central Park, lopsided structures built of cardboard, flattened gasoline tins, odd bits of lumber, broken furniture.

Although he himself was a hairsbreadth away from ending up in one of those hovels, he was among the fortunate ones. There was one job left, one opening he hadn't tried. They were looking for men to work on the new IND line. And thus he was saved.

But what about the others in that desolate shantytown? Surely they must have heard the sounds of the mayor celebrating in his Casino nearby. Surely some of them caught wind of a distant melody that seemed to be coming from beyond the trees.

"Will you still love me in December as you did in May?" a faint voice sang, plaintive and mocking.

On a bleak day in December, Jimmy Walker, looking fragile and worn, pays his last visit to City Hall before fleeing to Europe, where his mistress is waiting for him.

On the same day, a haggard-looking man makes his way from Central Park to a line of men seeking employment on the Independent subway. To his amazement, he ends up getting a job as a platform man, and although the pay is miserable and the hours are backbreakingly long, he can hold his head up again.

"Hell hath no fury like a Hylan scorned," Jimmy Walker quipped during his mayoral campaign. The subway under Walker was a subway blessedly free of the vindictive meddling of the Hylan years. When Walker came into office, he promised to provide more transit facilities without "political or personal interference," and he kept his word. The BMT could breathe more easily now: the vast Coney Island Yard and Repair Shop, for example, was finally completed, an urgently needed improvement that Hylan had systematically stalled. And at the same time, work on the municipal subway went forward, coming to fruition in the Eighth

Avenue line. (This was the most significant subway improvement of the Walker years, but the mayor didn't get a chance to savor it, setting sail for Europe twelve hours after the line was opened for service.)

Walker was a friend of the subway and he fought for it, but he wasn't above making backroom deals. He knew how to finesse a situation, when the need arose; in fact, he was very good at it. "No one could hold a candle to Jimmy when it came to charm," one of his mistresses once said of him. "When you looked into his eyes, all your problems melted away." And even the dour Judge Seabury, head of the corruption investigation, was warned not to make eye contact when he was interrogating him. In a famous photograph of the trial, Judge Seabury stares fixedly off into space, while Walker gazes quizzically into the room, as though he is a little surprised by the odd behavior of his questioner.

But Walker wasn't equipped to deal with the Great Depression, and ultimately the subway suffered for it. The son of Irish immigrants who turned to Tammany Hall when they were in trouble or out of a job, Walker did nothing to stop the Tammany machine from stealing money from the city. When Governor Franklin D. Roosevelt began sending aid to New York, Tammany took a huge portion of the desperately needed relief funds, and Walker looked the other way.

The subway seemed as mobbed as ever, but the truth was that ridership was in decline. In 1930, the first Depression year, unemployment in New York quadrupled. By the end of the year, there were 6,000 apple sellers in the city, crouching, in the words of Gene Fowler, like "half-remembered sins . . . on the conscience of the town."

One out of every six New Yorkers was out of work; in Harlem, it was one out of four. Two hundred thousand evictions were issued in 1931, and there were 15,000 homeless people on the streets. Far fewer people were riding the subway to work, and for many the nickel fare was prohibitive.

The extravagant projects undertaken by Hylan and Walker in the "golden boom" of the twenties had left the city reeling with debt. The subways added greatly to the strain—the Dual System was able to pay only a fraction of what it owed the city, forcing the city to draw on the tax budget to pay the debt. And the IND, which cost $9 million per route mile to build, 125 percent more than the earlier IRT and BMT, was an incredible expense, especially since the city had to underwrite its operating costs as well. By the 1930s, municipal operation of the IND had become a financial catastrophe. The city was paying nine cents on every nickel ride at a time when the true cost of a single ride was fourteen cents. The IRT went into receivership in 1932, falling into the vortex of the Depression. Starved of capital, its equipment breaking down, the transit industry was suffering.

Massive unemployment, paralysis, aching unrest, a city of breadlines, evictions, suicide, disease—this was the city that was taken on by Fiorello La Guardia, a little man who was larger than life. The son of an Italian father and an Austrian Jewish mother, La Guardia had worked as an interpreter in Serbo-Croatian on Ellis Island, an experience that he never forgot. He saw immigrants with nothing but the shirts on their backs detained for questioning day after day, without any assurance that they would be let in, and all because they spoke some village dialect no one could understand. And he saw others turned away because they had trachoma, an affliction of the eye, people who had staked everything on starting a new life only to have their hopes destroyed in the course of a three-minute medical exam.

"I contain multitudes," Walt Whitman said, affirming his connectedness to all human beings. More than any other, this phrase sums up Fiorello La Guardia's ambition. "How many languages do you speak?" he was once asked. "Yiddish, Italian, Ukrainian—whatever it takes."

Unlike Jimmy Walker, who was rarely glimpsed before noon, La Guardia was everywhere at once, scurrying up

Fiorello La Guardia, Al Smith, and Robert Moses at the opening of the Belt Parkway, 1938, with Smith's wife, Katie, behind Moses. Courtesy of MTA Bridges and Tunnels Special Archive

ladders and crawling down into tunnels, with a flock of reporters trotting after him. Dashing to fires, racing to train wrecks, confiscating guns, smashing slot machines and hurling them into the East River, he made New Yorkers feel that he was willing to go to the wall for them—provided they were on the up-and- up, and that they weren't just out for themselves.

When La Guardia first came into office, he compared himself to an artist or sculptor "who has a conception that he wishes to carve or paint, who has a model before him, but hasn't a chisel or brush." But from the beginning, he had the president's ear, an advantage he capitalized on. "He would fly to Washington at the drop of a hat," a close observer said, "and he always had a letter with him, the kind that breaks your heart. He'd read it out loud in this high, raspy voice. . . . It got to FDR every time."

Thanks to La Guardia's rapport with FDR, New York received more Work Projects Administration funds than any other city in the United States. "Red, white, and blue WPA signs showed up everywhere," one Brooklynite recalled, "and men with shovels were never far behind."

The subway received $23,160,000 from the WPA for the building of the IND. This was the first federal grant that had ever come its way, but it wasn't nearly enough. Once again, the subway was in crisis, a crisis that called for a complete restructuring. In La Guardia's mind, this meant only one thing—unification of all existing lines.

Like others before him, La Guardia believed that the city should run the subway itself, and that the subway could be self-supporting. A unified system would get rid of the Dual System's preferentials and allow interest costs and sinking fund charges to be paid out of subway revenues instead of by taxes. From the signing of the Dual Contracts in 1913, the city hadn't received any money from the BRT, and it had gotten only $19 million from the IRT. By combining the BRT, the IRT, and the Independent line under one management, La Guardia believed that the city would save millions of dollars.

Unification had been a recurrent theme ever since the Transit Commission first proposed it in 1921. Under La Guardia, it was finally agreed that the city would acquire the BMT subway, els, trolleys, and bus lines for $175 million and the IRT for $151 million, a purchase made possible by an amendment that excluded $315 million from the city's debt limit.

The agreement, which included dismantling the els, was celebrated à la La Guardia. On the twentieth of December, in 1939, the mayor put on a construction worker's helmet and face mask, both of which seemed too large for him. A transit worker handed him a blazing acetylene torch. Seizing the torch, the Little Flower cut through a beam, initiating the tearing down of the Sixth Avenue El.

But the destruction of the Sixth Avenue El struck fear into the hearts of many IRT employees, especially those that belonged to the Transport Workers Union, men like seventy-one-year-old Herman Klotsky. An IRT station agent for thirty-one years, Klotsky had a schedule as predictable as the mail—twelve hours a day, seven days a week, without a single vacation or holiday. And then, in 1937, thanks to the intervention of the TWU, he got a two-week vacation and paid holiday.

"For thirty-one years, I lived underground," Klotsky said. "It was as though I had finally come up for air." The union got him medical benefits as well, which made a huge difference in his life.

"A lot of us get ulcers," he explained. "You never eat right and you're always worried that something will go wrong." Thanks to his new contract, and the advice of an excellent doctor, his condition finally improved.

For workers like Klotsky, unification was bad news. And his fears were well founded, as it turned out. Under the Wickes Act of 1939, TWU workers would be civil servants—and according to a TWU broadside, this was the result:

> *Ten months ago the city paid $340,000,000 for the bankrupt private corporations which operated the subways and elevated railways. At that time, we were promised that we could get many things under civil service.*
> *What did we get?*

The writer proceeds to list the rights and benefits that have been snatched away.

> *Many transit workers had their pay cut. The seven day work week is being brought back. Hundreds of men have been laid off. Our seniority rights have been violated. Promotions guaranteed to us in contracts have been denied. Five to nine percent is being cut from our pay for pensions we have nothing to say about.*

The writer concludes with what he sees as the most ominous development of all:

> *The city is ruthlessly violating labor agreements. The right of labor to bargain collectively is being denied.*

The anger builds and builds, until finally Michael Quill, president of the TWU, puts all his outrage into one great cry that will be repeated by workers all over town. In an open letter to the mayor, Quill accuses La Guardia of betraying workers everywhere:

> *We asked you for bread and you gave us a stone. Thus do you turn against labor—you who have always pretended to be a staunch friend of labor, and, under that pretense, have achieved high place and power.*

In the same letter, Quill points to the tearing down of the Sixth Avenue El as evidence of what unification will bring.

Our own experience has shown that management under public ownership can be as cruel and ruthless as private management. Need we remind you of the inhuman treatment you inflicted upon the 600 men thrown on the scrap heap when the 6th Avenue El was demolished?

The TWU and the city had locked horns.

No one knew how the conflict would turn out.

After repeated threats of massive strikes, the city was forced to concede that the TWU had a right to engage in collective bargaining. Although a truce finally emerged, the union's confidence in La Guardia was badly damaged.

Apart from the humanitarian issue of its workers, another epoch-making event was taking place: the unification of the BRT, the IRT, and the IND—the greatest railroad merger in the history of the United States. With 500 rapid transit stations and 760 track miles of subways and els, it was truly spectacular, carrying 1.8 billion passengers in its first year of operation.

The last great surge of subway building took place in the depths of the Depression. One of the most dramatic feats of construction occurred at Herald Square. A new IND line was built over the Pennsylvania Railroad tubes and the Long Island Rail Road tubes and under the Broadway BMT and the Hudson and Manhattan tubes. Looking at diagrams of the construction is mind-boggling. At the time of construction, the Sixth Avenue elevated line was still operating above the new Sixth Avenue line, so this had to be supported, along with the heavy street traffic overhead, not to mention another complicating factor—a high-pressure water main that carried tons of water from Catskill mountain reservoirs into the city. ("It makes surgery look easy," an engineer remarked.) The Herald Square maze, with its lines snaking in and out, was finally completed in 1940. In December of that year, the first

trains began to run under Sixth Avenue from Fiftieth Street to West Fourth, the last major opening of the IND.

Everything about the subway was more streamlined now, from techniques of construction to the look of the cars and stations. But New York had fallen under the spell of the automobile, and a new charismatic figure appeared on the scene. A visionary, an elitist, a monomaniac, a man who would leave his fingerprints all over the city. A brooding man with veiled, slightly fishlike eyes—Robert Moses, master builder of New York.

Moses, it is often said, didn't care about people; he cared about cars. But the truth is he didn't even care about cars. He cared about movement—motion—getting there. Preserving the character of old buildings and neighborhoods was far less important to him than providing scenic "ribbon parks" that could be admired in passing, from the windows of a speeding car. With a brilliance matched by burning ambition, Moses dominated New York's bridges, tunnels, and roadways for almost fifty years.

He began by creating a network of limited-access roads that led out to Long Island, taking over the process of decentralization that the subway had begun, and then he went on to transform the city itself, restoring its crumbling public parks—he completed 1,700 renovation projects in 1934 alone—and creating new playgrounds—in nonblack neighborhoods. And then came the jewel in the crown, the mighty Triborough Bridge, three bridges in one. Public money poured into Moses' projects—a quarter billion dollars were spent on the West Side Improvement, a series of highway and park projects extending from lower Manhattan all the way up through the Bronx to the Saw Mill River Parkway, and 31 million man-hours were put into the Triborough Bridge.

But Moses didn't anticipate what Parsons, the great engineer of the subway, saw right away—that each new conduit would create a new circulation crisis, that each new road would be hopelessly backed up with cars.

The Triborough Bridge opened in July of 1936, and it was hailed as one of the greatest engineering achievements the world had ever seen. But in August of the same year, the parkways of Long Island suffered the worst traffic jam in the history of New York.

Moses' solution was to build more and more roads, but the congestion problem was never solved. And all this time, Moses was consolidating his power, creating an empire of his own. Invoking legislation he had drafted himself, he set up the Triborough Bridge and Tunnel Authority, using revenues from tolls to fund projects at his own discretion.

In all of Moses' schemes, the car was given the place of pride, and the subway was stripped of its prestige, toiling in a new obscurity.

On June 15, 1936, an army of workers gathered in Flushing Meadows, a little-known spot far out in Queens that the *New York Times* described as "one part ash dump and two parts marshes." In three short years, this wasteland was transformed into the site of the 1939 World's Fair, an extravaganza orchestrated by Robert Moses.

"Out of the Darkness of the Depression Arises a Vision of Hope," read a caption underneath a photograph of the fair's giant emblems, the Trylon and the Perisphere. The subway carried millions of people out to the site; the IRT and the BMT had World's Fair trains, and a spur was added to the IND, leading through the Flushing Yard to the World's Fair Station near Horace Harding Boulevard. Agnes Encosi of Harlem remembered going to the World's Fair as a little girl.

My whole family rode out there on the Flushing line, myself, my parents, and my big brother.

"We're going to see the future," my brother Ezra said. We were all dressed up in our Sunday best and so was everybody else on that train. The next thing I remember is getting out and seeing that ball and needle up in the sky. It was like they were floating, as big as they were, and the whole place was shiny, like it was plated with silver and gold.

The Futurama was the star attraction, but it was scary to me. You sat on these little sofas that moved along an invisible track, and you looked down on a huge model of mountains and valleys and lakes with grey ribbons that were highways cutting through. There were tiny houses sitting on the hills, pretty houses with fences around them. But the city looked lonely and sad—it was all big skyscrapers and wide, wide roads, not just four lanes but maybe ten or twelve, and you couldn't see any sidewalks anywhere.

"That's what New York is gonna look like when we grow up," my brother said to me.

"But where can we play?" I wanted to know, because all the kids that I knew played on the street. Ezra laughed and said that when the future came, you wouldn't need the streets because everybody would have a car.

The look of that city made me sad, and that night, after we got home, I prayed to God that the future would never come.

Between 1939 and 1940, the subway carried millions of visitors to the World's Fair, transporting them beyond the stern realities of the Depression to a technological utopia. Once the visitors passed through the Art Deco gates, the subway was largely forgotten.

For better or worse, the future seemed to lie in the car, an assumption that was already transforming—and undoing—the city.

CHAPTER SEVEN

From GI Joe to Jackie Robinson

Help Scrap the Axis
By Placing Iron and Metal Scrap on the Curb!

The More You Give, the More Will Live:
Your Red Cross Is at His Side

Give that they may Live
Save Food
Give Cash
Now

T hus the subway began its wartime service, with one poster campaign after another reminding citizens of their obligations, imploring them to be patriotic, and cautioning them to be discreet. For no one knew just what dangers lay ahead.

LOOSE LIPS SINK SHIPS
UNCLE SAM WANTS YOU!

Crowd of passengers boarding BMT Standard during World War II, circa 1943. NYTM

Soldiers flooded the city (two million of them) on their way to war. Eager for a night on the town, they crowded into the subway, where—at least according to the movies—they fell in love.

Grand Central Station, 1941: a man (Robert Walker) and a woman (Judy Garland) gaze at one another on the crowded platform of the downtown IRT. But the next moment, the crowd sweeps the woman into the subway car, and the number 6 train rolls out before the soldier can reach her. Beside himself, he boards the next train, taking it to Fourteenth Street, while the woman, pacing back and forth, waits for him at Thirty-third. *He's an out-of-towner!* she suddenly realizes, stopping dead in her tracks. *He won't know the difference between the local and the express!*

"The subway was filled with soldiers in those days," a former token booth operator recalled, "and a lot of them came straight off the farm. They didn't have a clue about how to get from A to B, and they didn't have a whole lot of time."

But the soldier in our movie (*The Clock*) is a quick study. He finds his girl and they get married at City Hall. As the judge rattles off the words of the wedding vow, the roar of an el drowns out his voice—the train is the movie's secret star.

Crowd of passengers, including many in service uniforms, pushing through turnstiles into IRT station during World War II, circa 1943. NYTM

In memoirs of the war period, a new image of the subway emerges: it had become a communal place. It was a time of crisis, and straphangers drew together as never before. Strangers discussed the headlines they were reading over each other's shoulders. And rumors spread like wildfire. The subway was target number one in a Nazi plot to paralyze New York. The subway would be used as a shelter in an air raid. The entire city would go underground.

The subway wasn't just the subway anymore. Both in people's imaginations and in reality, it was part of a national struggle for survival. From 1940 to 1945, the subway became part of the war effort in countless ways.

For one thing, the American military needed all the steel and rubber it could get. The auto industry ground to a halt, and the drivers crowded into the trains. Subway cars were packed to capacity—and beyond, people complained, saying that the overcrowding was unbearable.

Such complaints, however, were music to the mayor's ears.

"Overcrowding?" La Guardia exclaimed to the group of reporters that was always running at his heels. Haggard and worn, this exhausted wartime mayor was seen to break into a gleeful smile. "Anytime we don't have crowding during rush hour, there'll be a receiver sitting in the mayor's chair and New York will be a ghost town. Why, they talk about rush hour and the crash and the noise. Why, listen, don't you see that's proof of our life and vitality? Why, why, this is New York City!"

V-Day, August 1945. The trains were crowded as never before. Millions of people flooded into Times Square, as though an irresistible force was drawing them together. The celebration started in the subways—passengers danced in the aisles, cried on each other's shoulders, and broke into drunken song. All night long, the trains indulged the delirious crowds, and when the sun rose over the East River, it was the subway that carried them home.

Subway poster for the Red Cross, circa 1943: "This Year We Must Give More / Your Red Cross Is at His Side." NYTM

"There were no strangers on the trains," one woman recalled. "It was like the whole city belonged to us."

Reenter Robert Moses, with his vision and his egotism and his lack of humanity in the service of humanity—because, after all, he did see what he was doing as being in the service of humanity.

As soon as the war was over, Moses unveiled an $82 million plan for miles and miles of highways and bridges—but where was the money going to come from?

In 1945, New York needed many things that had gone neglected during the war. It needed hospitals and schools and libraries. It needed sewers. And especially, *it needed subway lines.*

The truth was that the subway was in terrible trouble. Even the heavily used subway of World War II was running under a deficit, resulting in the cutting back of greatly needed development. (The Second Avenue subway was a case in point: the plans had been gathering dust in a city engineer's drawer since World War I. Now that the Second Avenue El had been torn down, a Second Avenue line was more critical than ever.)

The new mayor, William O'Dwyer, a rugged Irishman from County Mayo, was instantly flooded with demands.

Everyone wanted something, and they wanted it *now.* Where was the money going to come from? O'Dwyer had served as a policeman, a lawyer, a magistrate, and a judge, but nothing had prepared him for this. He had the support of Robert Moses, the backing of Tammany Hall, and some mob connections that would eventually come to light, but raw power wasn't enough to untie the intricate knot that had been placed in his hands.

The problems of the subway were the most pressing of all. The subway deficit—$37 million in 1944—was putting a great strain on the city's postwar economy. For Paul Windels, a Republican lawyer who had served as an adviser to La Guardia, the solution was as clear as day.

Raise the fare to ten cents, Windels said, and not only would you pay off the deficit, you would be able to provide the municipal treasury with $10 million every year. A ten-cent fare would cover the cost of new aluminum cars, not to mention air-conditioning.

Soldier resting on rattan seat in IRT car, circa 1943. NYTM

The nickel fare wasn't honest, Windels claimed, it was hopelessly political. It was time to take the politics out of mass transit and to run it like a clean, efficient, rationally organized business. To lobby for a ten-cent fare, Windels created the Citizens Transit Commission, a powerful group of businessmen and realtors who resented the fact that the subway was indirectly raising property taxes.

And then Robert Moses threw his weight behind the ten-cent fare, increasing the pressure on Mayor O'Dwyer. But councilman Stanley Isaacs, former borough president of Manhattan, publicly challenged Moses' motives, something most New York politicians were extremely reluctant to do.

Isaacs went on a campaign to let New Yorkers know why Moses was so keen on raising the fare. The subway was swallowing an enormous portion of the city's funds—funds that Moses coveted for his own projects. The future of mass transit meant very little to Robert Moses; for him, the car was everything, and the subway nothing.

"Why should the straphanger who doesn't own a car subsidize the motorist?" Isaacs asked indignantly in an article written in 1946. "So that the city will be able to borrow more money to build parkways, expressways, and highways, which are to be furnished free of charge . . . to the man who can afford his own car, doesn't travel on the subways, and doesn't pay even a nickel toward the construction of the speedways furnished him."

Isaacs lashed out against the Citizens Transit Commisssion, saying that its recommendations were driven by self-interest. Once upon a time, realtors had eagerly followed subway lines, but now they were following highways instead. The very same realtors who had capitalized on the nickel fare were now clamoring for a ten-cent fare in the name of the automobile.

Isaacs took his campaign to the radio, trying to make New Yorkers see what doubling the fare would mean for the city's poor. A difference of a few pennies would be sharply felt, cutting into basic necessities. "It will mean less milk for growing children," he told his listeners. "It will mean thinner coats for those same children when the weather gets cold."

In the end, the tide was turned by Michael Quill, the fiery leader of the TWU.

Quill was a fierce defender of the nickel fare, arguing that a fare hike would benefit large property owners at the expense of the working class. So when O'Dwyer's office began pressuring him to change his position, Quill dug in his heels.

Now, O'Dwyer and Quill were personal friends— according to Quill's wife, Shirley, there was a "deep affection" between the two men. "Fond as they both were of a bottle of Scotch," she wrote in her memoirs, "as they downed a quart, the mayor from Mayo grew ever more sentimental, while the thrush from Kerry warbled only slightly off-key, the familiar songs of Ireland's noble struggles."

Did they talk politics when they got together, or did they leave it by the door? All we know is that when it came to the nickel fare, O'Dwyer couldn't get Quill to change his mind.

But there were other forces acting on Michael Quill as leader of the TWU. After the war, he was under tremendous pressure to obtain a wage raise for the transit workers. His own authority, his own leadership, was on the line: he couldn't afford to let the Transport Workers Union down.

Some said that the transit system was in such dire financial straits that the only way to get a wage raise would be to double the fare. The skeptics warned the union not to be fooled: there was no reason to assume that the added revenues would find their way into the workers' pockets.

As the weeks went by, Quill was increasingly torn— and then it turned out that O'Dwyer wanted something

else from him as well. He wanted him to purge the TWU of Communist influence, despite the fact that Quill had worked closely with the Communist Party since the 1930s, when the TWU was formed.

And now Quill, who had come under increasing attack from the leftist elements in the TWU, had to make a choice between his principles and his position as negotiator in chief for the TWU, a job he believed he could do better than anyone else. If Quill secured a fare hike for his workers where the Communists who held key posts in the TWU had failed, the party's influence would be greatly weakened and his own position would be secured.

As for O'Dwyer, he was under pressure too. It was 1948, one year before election time. Rumor had it that the Communists were going to make the five-cent fare into the crux of the mayoral race. If he could find a way to push through the ten-cent fare with the blessing of Mike Quill, he would be in a much stronger position.

No one knows exactly what words were exchanged between "the mayor from Mayo" and "the thrush from Kerry" behind closed doors. All we know is that a deal was struck. After years of resistance, Quill agreed to the ten-cent fare, and O'Dwyer agreed to a twenty-four-cent-an-hour wage increase.

And then, on April 28, 1948, a drama was elaborately staged, scripted, no doubt, by Quill, who was once described by a *New York Times* labor writer as "a showman on a par with Jimmy Cagney or John Wayne." TWU leaders, many of whom were anti-Quill, were invited to a closed-door meeting in City Hall. A negotiating committee of three hundred men, composed of anti-Quill leftists and pro-Quill union members, were called in as observers.

The mayor turned to Quill and asked him what he needed from him in exchange for a no-strike pledge.

"Twenty-four cents an hour," Quill replied, which struck many in the room as an outrageously high increase.

"It's yours," O'Dwyer replied, taking everyone's breath away.

The pro-Quill members were overjoyed; the anti-Quill members knew they were beaten. Twenty-four cents was more than any transit union in the United States had been able to secure for years.

Thanks to this performance, Quill's position was solidified, and the transit workers were jubilant. Five thousand workers gathered in mid-May to celebrate their victory.

A week earlier, Mayor O'Dwyer had done what no other mayor had done before. Already knowing he had Quill in his corner, he had announced the ten-cent fare for subways and elevateds. The ten-cent fare went into effect on July 1, and the subway nickel, a New York institution for almost forty-five years, became a piece of history.

Although the politicians had turned it inside out, the subway was still called upon to support the people of New York both at work and at play, and this is reflected movingly in the seven glorious seasons between 1947 and 1956 when New York dominated major league baseball.

For seven seasons between 1947 and 1956, two New York teams competed for the world championship. The Yankees played in every one of these seven series, the

Passengers on River Avenue, the Bronx, Yankee Stadium, circa 1940. NYTM

ENJOY N.Y.'S SUMMER FESTIVAL

The Subway Sun
NEW YORK CITY TRANSIT AUTHORITY
Vol. XXII   No. 8

DODGERS YANKS GIANTS

a token takes you to SPORTS

Subway car poster, *The Subway Sun*, vol. XXII, no. 8, circa 1955. NYTM

Brooklyn Dodgers played in six, the New York Giants played in one. To the despair of some and the rapture of others, the mighty Yankees bested the National League team six times. The Yankees lost to the Dodgers in 1955, creating what one fan described as "a New Orleans chaos" on Brooklyn streets.

During these seasons, in Roger Angell's words, "baseball was the private possession of New York City." Cabbies, cops, businessmen, kids on the streets—everyone had a stake in it. And the subway was still the best way of getting to and from Yankee Stadium, Ebbet's Field, the Polo Grounds. Whether you were a Dodgers fan, a Giants fan, or a Yankees fan, the subway was there to carry you from the aggravations of daily life to the oasis of the ballpark.

And even if you couldn't get away, by stepping into the subway you were stepping into a place where the latest baseball news was being hotly followed.

"Everybody seemed to ride the subways," Arthur Richman, a *Daily Mirror* reporter, recalled. "There were kids with Giants caps, with Yankee caps, people with brown bags with their lunch going to games."

The age of coast-to-coast television broadcasting was already taking its toll on city stadiums. More and more fans were content to watch the games at home, and others were abandoning their old neighborhoods and moving out to the suburbs. But for the moment, a moment that was miraculously prolonged, baseball lifted the spirit of the city.

Jackie Robinson is at the plate. Here comes the pitch . . . and there goes a line drive to left field. The left-fielder stands back . . . leaps . . . it's over his head . . . against the wall. The man on second is rounding third. He's coming home . . . he scores. Brooklyn wins! The crowds are cheering wildly in the stands, crowds brought to the ballpark by courtesy of—who else?—the subway!

CHAPTER EIGHT

Dark Times

And I'll tell you another thing. *Never*—and I repeat—
never will New Yorkers pay to descend into a subway
hole," a famous journalist included among his yearly pre-
dictions in 1901. But they did descend. And what's more,
they embraced the subway. A second city was born under
the streets.

But by the 1960s and 1970s, after years and years of
neglect, the system was finally coming apart, unleashing
primal fears of the underground.

Sparks catching on piles of debris, filling the tunnels
with smoke; cars breaking down in the middle of runs; trains
veering off worn-out rails; 170, 180 emergencies reported
on any given day: fires, derailments, robberies, delays.

"There was no money," a former maintainer recalled.
"There was no funding to do anything. I remember my
supervisor telling me to go out into the lots and find
pieces of scrap plywood to nail up on a wall to shut up a
door because you couldn't find any plywood in the system."

And while transit workers struggled to keep an ailing
system up and running, the experience of riding the subway often seemed surreal. Speakers droned out warnings
no one could understand; riders stood stranded on crumbling platforms; graffiti covered every inch of wall.

Train pulling into 68th Street station, circa 1980. NYTM

"It was bad in the subway, and it was bad in the street," a former shopkeeper from East Tremont, a condemned section of the Bronx, remarked. Above ground, neighborhood after neighborhood was being destroyed to make way for the highways of Robert Moses.

Prior to the war, Moses had left his mark on regions outlying the city. After the war, he began, in the words of Robert Caro, "to paint on the most crowded canvas in the world: New York City." There are no better words to describe what this entailed than those provided by Moses himself, who unabashedly reveals his lack of concern for the common man.

You can draw any kind of picture you like on a clean slate and indulge your every whim in the wilderness in laying out a New Delhi, Canberra or Brasilia, but when

you operate in an overbuilt metropolis, you have to hack your way with a meat ax.

In the words of Bernard Malamud, "In New York, who needs the atom bomb? If you walked away from a place, they tore it down."

By fiat of Robert Moses, a quarter of a million New Yorkers were displaced, many of them ending up in desolate housing projects. And then there were those who tried desperately to hold out—elderly people who had lived in their apartments for forty or fifty years, now living in terror behind locked doors while neighboring flats were being gutted and demolished.

Bridges leapt across rivers, highways interlaced the boroughs, but on countless streets that had once been teeming with life there was nothing but misery and violence. It was the age of the evacuation notice and the wrecking ball—and it was the darkest hour of the New York subway.

While the city was being reinvented for the automobile—the total cost of roads built by Moses after the war was over $32 billion—the development of the subway ground to a complete halt. By 1960, not a single mile of subway track had been laid for twenty years. In 1974, as Robert Caro points out, "people using subways and railroads were still riding on tracks laid between 1904 and 1933, the last year before Robert Moses came to power." And although the original construction of the subway was superb, its tracks, stations, and cars had fallen into shocking disrepair.

Once upon a time, the subway had been New York's pride and joy. How hard that was to remember now.

Mayor Robert Wagner, a U.S. senator's son who had grown up in the world of politics, promised that he would set things straight. "New York Needs More than a Token Mayor," one of his campaign buttons declared. Publicity

Passengers waiting on the 14th Street station platform, March 27, 1970. Photo by Photo Communications Co., Inc.

Mayor Robert F. Wagner and company in new R-33 or R-36 "World's Fair" subway car, circa 1964. NYTM

photos captured the mayor riding the subway with glamorous friends, but the balance of power didn't change. For the three terms Wagner served as mayor, Robert Moses continued to call the shots when it came to transportation in the city.

Wagner did make good on his promise to put a police officer on every train, increasing the ranks of the Transit Police to 2,900, a threefold expansion of the existing force. But as working-class communities were razed to the ground and middle-class New Yorkers moved out to the suburbs, a chasm opened up between the rich and the poor, and urban crime continued to soar. As chief of police Meehan observed at a conference in 1981, crimes in the subway aroused a special kind of terror.

The subway isn't Greenwich Village or Coney Island or Harlem or the South Bronx. The subway is all those places . . . the transit system is everybody's neighborhood. If a New Yorker lives in Brooklyn, he may not care about a crime that occurs in the streets in the Bronx or Queens, but if he rides the subway every day he cares very much if the same crime occurs in the subway anywhere in the city. In a real sense, the whole system is his neighborhood.

With the city reeling from the destruction of old neighborhoods above ground, the violation of its underground neighborhood was more traumatic than ever.

Enter John Vliet Lindsay, tall and handsome, with Waspy good looks—a "matinee idol," Moses sneered—full of energy, optimism, and lofty ideals. Moses was old now, seventy-seven, and for the first time in his forty years of power the mayor of New York made no secret of wanting him out. LINDSAY MAPS PLANS TO SQUASH MOSES' POWER, a headline read. "The city is for people, not automobiles," Lindsay proclaimed. The subway would help to bring the city back, breathing new life into dying neighborhoods.

"We're going to make our subway work again," Lindsay vowed at a campaign rally. "Does anybody remember that $500 million transit bond that was supposed to be used to build a new Second Avenue line? Well, under Bob Wagner, the system had gotten so bad that the money had to be used for fixing tracks and cars. Under John Lindsay, we will continue to fix tracks and cars—*and* we'll get air-conditioning"—wild cheers—"*and* we'll build the Second Avenue line."

While Lindsay promised miracles, his nemesis, Michael Quill, stood scowling in the wings. Short and balding, the leader of the Transport Workers Union was the very antithesis of the dazzling young politician. An Irish rebel against British rule who had been forced to flee to this country without a penny to his name, Quill had no patience for Lindsay, with his idealism and his expensive suits. People were hailing Lindsay as "the Republican

Subway track work and third rail welding on the D line, circa 1954. NYTM

Kennedy," but to Quill he seemed arrogant—and wet behind the ears.

"New York is a proud city," Lindsay said in a campaign speech, "and the subway is part of what makes us great." But the very first day he came into office, he was hit with a massive transit strike.

Several weeks earlier, reporters and radio broadcasters had crowded into a conference room at the Brooklyn headquarters of the Transit Authority to hear Quill lay out the demands of the union.

"Our requests are so light," he had said with a genial shrug, "that the Transit Authority shouldn't have any trouble granting them by early December."

"That's not what we've heard!" a reporter put in. Quill looked at him mildly and went on.

"We want half-pay pensions after twenty-five years of service, regardless of age. We want six weeks of vacation after one year of service."

"Why not ask for a paid vacation on the Riviera?" a radio broadcaster quipped.

"That's not for this strike, that's for the next," Quill is said to have replied. "We want a four-day, thirty-two-hour workweek with no loss of pay—and we're going to get it too."

"There isn't enough gold in Fort Knox to pay this bill!" the opposition exclaimed when it was presented with the TWU's demands.

It was now November of 1965, and the strike deadline was set for January 1. What would Lindsay do when he stepped into Wagner's place? The suspense was building all over town.

"What will your response be?" reporters were pressing him.

"I have nothing to say. Try me tomorrow," he would reply, flashing them a charming smile.

"Lindsley [Quill insisted on getting his name wrong] claims to be the champion of the subway," Quill told the press. "But I actually care about the people who make it run."

When Lindsay suggested that the strike deadline be pushed back, Quill asked for "less profile and more courage" from the mayor-elect.

By the time Lindsay finally came to the table, he and Quill were already enemies. Lindsay associated Quill with the politics of backroom deals; Quill associated Lindsay with the silk-stocking district of Park Avenue and the power elite. As Jimmy Breslin put it, "John Lindsay looked at Quill and he saw the past. And Mike Quill looked at Lindsay and he saw the Church of England."

Thus matters stood on the last day before the strike, December 31, 1965. The scene of the battle wasn't Gracie Mansion, it was a ballroom at the Americana Hotel, where Lindsay was currently staying. (Lindsay had bitterly offended Wagner, who had just lost his wife, by telling reporters that Gracie Mansion was a mess and that it wasn't fit to move into yet.)

The negotiations went on all through the day, with Lindsay attending, tense, determined, and impeccably dressed. Quill, who had recently grown thin and frail as a result of a serious heart condition, was wearing a suit that had seen him through many fights, but it didn't fit him properly, hanging loosely from his bony frame.

The Transit Authority presented the union with a compromise package that it considered generous.

"Is this some kind of a joke?" one of the union members barked.

"Peanuts!" another chimed in. The "peanut package," as it was called from then on, threw Quill into a rage. Although the package came from the Transit Authority, he blamed Lindsay for its meagerness.

"We'll take no more bubkes from a schmuck like you!" Quill thundered at Lindsay in his heaviest brogue.

"Well, that was a nice statement from the union," Lindsay replied. "Now let's hear from the other side."

As the clock raced toward midnight, Lindsay rose to his feet and implored the union not to strike. In a magnanimous gesture, he invited everyone to come up to his suite, saying he was willing to go on negotiating until dawn.

With the deadline only minutes away, Michael Quill thumped his walking stick on the floor, pointed a gnarled finger at Lindsay, and shouted with all his might, "You are a juvenile, a lightweight, and a pip-squeak! You have to grow up! You don't know anything about the working class and you don't know anything about labor unions!"

During this tirade, Lindsay was very still, but he was trembling. Struggling for self-mastery, he finally spoke, gripping the edge of the table.

"I don't mind your words about me personally," he managed to get out. "But I will not have you addressing the office of the mayor that way. It is an affront to the people of New York."

Quill got up disgustedly, knocking over a glass of water, his face twisted into a mask of fury. It was just past midnight: negotiations had come to an end. Lindsay was now officially the mayor.

At five o'clock the following morning, 34,000 transit workers went on strike, shutting down the subway and the bus lines for the first time in New York's history.

On the first day of the strike, Lindsay begged New Yorkers to stay home, and only a quarter of the 3.2 million who usually entered Manhattan reported to their jobs. By the second day, people were ignoring his pleas and the streets and highways were choked with cars.

On the second day, a ruling came down that Michael Quill and other leaders of the TWU would be sent to jail for civil contempt of court. Quill strode into the ballroom of the Americana Hotel, where camera crews and reporters were waiting for him.

"The judge can drop dead in his black robes," Quill declared defiantly. "I don't care if I rot in jail. I will not call off this strike."

Two hours after arriving at the prison, Quill suffered congestive heart failure. Rumor had it that Lindsay had refused to let Quill have his medicine in jail. Quill was transferred to Bellevue Hospital. ("Is he play-acting?" a reporter asked one of Quill's doctors, as though, even now, Quill was simply obeying his superb sense of timing.)

TWU demonstrators during 1966 transit strike. Robert F. Wagner Labor Archives, New York University. Photograph by Sam Reiss

While Quill lay in the hospital, the strike dragged on, and traffic tightened its stranglehold on the city. Although no one was allowed to visit Quill, Richard Price, a close adviser to the mayor, was finally admitted into his room. The attending doctor removed Quill's oxygen tank just long enough for the sick man to hold up four fingers—indicating that the strike would end when a four-day workweek was obtained.

After twelve days, Lindsay capitulated to the TWU, agreeing to a settlement worth an estimated $43 to $70 million. Two weeks later, Quill died of congestive heart failure, having helped to obtain the largest pay increase—a 15 percent wage hike to be spread out over two years—that had ever been awarded to a union in the United States.

Three thousand transport workers filed into St. Patrick's Cathedral to pay their last respects to a man who had become their hero. His casket was draped in an Irish Republican Army flag, leading one Irishman to whisper to another, "Do you remember those stories Mike used to tell about the troubles in Ireland when he was a boy?"

"He drank in rebellion with his mother's milk," the other replied.

The mourners proceeded from St. Patrick's to the cemetery, only to come up against a cemetery workers' picket line. When they saw Quill's casket, the cemetery workers flung open the gates, taking off their hats as the procession went by.

In the words of the English poet William Blake, "there is no friendship without opposition," and after the strike Lindsay and Quill made their peace. Quill said that he had called Lindsay "a pip-squeak and an amateur in the heat of battle and under war conditions," and that the time for those kinds of words was past. Two days later, Quill was dead, and Lindsay paid tribute to him. "Michael Quill's death marks the end of an era," Lindsay wrote. "He was a man who was very much part of New York."

When the dust had settled, everyone in New York had an opinion about Lindsay's handling of the strike. Some said he should have capitulated right away, pointing out that his principles had cost the city an estimated $6 million a day in lost taxes and money spent on overtime for city workers. Others said Lindsay had been too soft, and that he never should have agreed to such a handsome settlement, setting a dangerous precedent.

But there was one lesson the strike brought home more powerfully than ever before: for all the romance of the car, the subway was the lifeblood of the city.

CHAPTER NINE

The Subway Makes a Comeback

I n the early 1980s, David Gunn, head of the Philadelphia Transit System, is taken on a tour of the Coney Island Yard. He asks many questions, more than the workers are accustomed to, listening to their answers with growing astonishment. When Gunn talks to the press afterward, there is a note of outrage in his voice.

"The working conditions are atrocious," he says to them. "I felt depressed for the people in the shop. They're standing in muck. The roof leaks. They don't have the parts. The place has the atmosphere of absolute neglect."

When one of the reporters quizzes him about the presidency of the TA—everyone knows Gunn is being courted by Robert Kiley, chairman of the MTA, a man who has sworn that he will bring the subway back—Gunn's answer is like a slap in the face.

"It would be a suicide mission," he replies, a remark that gets quoted everywhere.

The subway was like a giant in chains. What was it that had brought the system down? Ask transit workers with twenty

Graffiti-covered R-33 subway car, circa 1980. NYTM

or thirty years of experience under their belts, and each one has a different story to tell.

"It was the fiscal crisis of the seventies, and the loss of city jobs," a motorman says. "We lost a quarter of our ridership."

Everyone has an opinion, a diagnosis—X, Y, or Z was at the bottom of the crisis.

"It was that retirement plan that Quill pushed through," a supervisor says, shaking his head. "On account of that plan, we lost many of our best men. They retired! Why should they keep going after twenty years when they could get half pay, regardless of age?" (Seventy percent of the skilled workers in the car maintenance program alone retired between July 1968 and June 1970.)

"It was the R44s and the R46s," a machinist remarks. "They cost the system an arm and a leg. State of the art, the wave of the future, the cat's meow—and then it turned out that they had major structural flaws, and we didn't have the technology in place to deal with them."

The truth is that there was no single cause; it took years of neglect to bring a great system down. And once the system was on its knees, there were those who said that its predicament was inevitable, implying that there was nothing to be done.

And of course the trend-watchers had to put their two cents in as well, going on and on in their jargonistic way: "The dilemma of the New York subway is the logical out-

come of irreversible tendencies that . . ." etc., etc., citing the suburbanization of America, the shortening of the workweek—gloom and doom.

Had the best days of the subway really come and gone? Would the system ever get back on its feet?

By 1984, a front-page article in the *New York Times* was calling the subway a system "in radical decline," pointing to "antiquated tracks, flawed rolling stock, water seepage in tunnels"—the list of failings went on and on. While some say that such exposés were overdone, others will tell you they were telling it like it was.

"The cars were so bad in those days," Joe Hofmann, former senior vice president of New York City Transit, recalls. "All the cars were covered with graffiti. You couldn't find a train in the system where all the doors worked. Every three days we had a derailment."

Although it was still managing to serve 990 million passengers in 1982, the subway's behavior had become irrational. There was no predicting what it would do next.

"The subway system is having a nervous breakdown," warned Kiley in 1984, "not to mention all the people who struggle with using it. Even if the nervous breakdown is partly a problem of frazzled nerves, and even if there's medicine you can provide for the patient that makes it a little easier in the short run, a nervous breakdown usually signifies much deeper problems. And I think we've got them in the subway system."

In 1981, Richard Ravitch, chairman of the MTA, had declared the subway to be in a state of emergency, appealing to the state legislature for funds. In a brilliant move, he had proposed a Five-Year Capital Improvement Program, to be financed through the sale of a $6.3 billion bond.

While this daring proposal was being disputed in offices and courts, Ravitch came under increasing attack. An elegant man who wore expensive suits and got around

Graffiti removal. NYTM

town in a chauffeured limousine, it was all too easy to blame him for what one editorial described as our "filthy, inadequately ventilated, crime-plagued and graffiti-disfigured subway." Few people realized that behind the scenes, he was fighting for the subway's life.

The proposal finally went through in 1982, despite serious doubts as to whether the system could heal itself. But money—in this case, $6.3 billion—often brings as many problems as it solves. Like honey drawing flies, it attracted both honest construction firms and competing demolition crews, along with swindlers, con men, and sharks who made wild promises they could never deliver. It financed rebuilding programs that revealed hidden layers of decay. And it drew the press, who watched, carped, and criticized at every turn: Where was all that money going? Where were the improvements? What was the public getting for its bonds? Results were not immediately visible, and not only the public but also the legislators up north in Albany were unhappy.

With ridership falling, a campaign would have to be mounted on many fronts, behind the scenes and in full view of the cameras. Who could oversee this herculean task, which would involve every department of the system's bureaucracy? The transit world was in a state of suspense—and then David Gunn surprised everyone by accepting Robert Kiley's offer.

"Success is by no means assured," the forty-six-year-old Bostonian now told the press, "but I intend to do my damnedest." Whatever it was that made Gunn change his mind, the New York subway became his personal obsession.

Although he was Harvard-educated and given to wearing pinstripes and tweed, Gunn had no interest in ruling from on high. A man overflowing with vital energy and zeal, he not only rode the subway every day but made his presence known throughout the system.

"My real interaction with Mr. Gunn came when I was superintendent for Manhattan," Art Bethell recalls.

It came down that he wanted Grand Central Passageway cleaned up. If you remember that old Grand Central passageway from the shuttle to the Lexington Avenue line, there were barricades and plyboard rooms, old beat-up concessions and everything in there. The passageway was only six feet wide—today it's forty-five feet—because it was taken up with these temporary rooms. He decided he wanted all that cleaned up.

Now Mr. Gunn went through that passageway every morning because he went to MTA headquarters on Madison Avenue. So every day he'd come through there. And every day he'd come looking for me.

"Arty, where are you?" he'd call out to me. "I know you're here somewhere."

"I'm here, Boss. I'm here!"

—which became the song heard throughout the system as Gunn poked his nose into everything.

Revitalizing the system was a treacherous task, because it wasn't only a matter of overhauling trains and rehabilitating stations and repairing tracks. Changes also had to be made in management, and these changes came at a tremendous cost.

One of Gunn's most controversial moves was to remove union protection and Civil Service from top supervisors, vastly increasing the power of management.

"We had a union that controlled a lot of what was going on," Jerry Skinner, a manager at the Coney Island Yard, explains. "The old hat was the supervisor. The supervisor had a union. The foremen had a union. Every level had a union."

The managers were given more power and the union was cut back, unleashing a storm of criticism. Who was right and who was wrong? Gunn insisted that these measures were justified.

"Too many supervisors are protected by the Civil Service, which drastically curtails the prerogative of the TA president," he told the press. If he was to succeed in the prodigious task of turning the system around, he needed to be free to pick people to do a job—and to dismiss them if they failed.

Some lost their jobs, others moved up; some were forced out of the system, others were given breaks that made their careers. Some claimed they were victims of the Kiley-Gunn regime; others believed that chaos had finally been replaced with a rationally organized system of management.

Who was right and who was wrong? Were the hirings and firings always fair? Transit workers still debate these questions today, but there is one point that almost everyone agrees upon. It was Gunn, with Kiley backing him up, who saw to it that workers were given what they needed to do their jobs—parts, tools, materials—and, above all, decent working conditions.

Take a tour of the Coney Island Yard: the "absolute neglect" that Gunn found there is long gone. Beneath the clanging of the great machines, there is a sense of concentration and calm. In this vast beehive of activity—the Coney Island Shop is the largest rapid-transit heavy-repair shop in the Northern Hemisphere—nothing is left to chance.

Trains are taken apart, cleaned, inspected, and put together again according to a strict, time-based schedule. Before the Gunn era, parts were replaced when they broke down, and the replacement parts were often in shaky condition. Kiley described seeing "the undercarriages of cars laboriously stripped down and being rebuilt with the same old nuts and bolts and component parts that had just been taken out—which is the same as subjecting yourself to the trauma and expense of a heart transplant only to wake up and discover that the doctor put your old, damaged heart back into place."

Components now get replaced *before* they break down, in accordance with the Scheduled Maintenance System (SMS) that was implemented under Gunn. Although this innovation escaped the notice of the general public, it revolutionized the operations of the Coney Island Yard and ultimately changed the experience of riding the subway.

"Now all the cars are running well," Joe Hofmann observes, praising the changes implemented by Gunn. "We have the highest performance in the world in our Maintenance Shop."

But while these changes were being achieved behind the scenes, the public needed a visible sign that the system was being taken in hand. And the legislators in Albany needed evidence as well, especially since the MTA was going to ask for more federal money, to the tune of $8 billion.

In order to gain credibility, Gunn mounted an all-out campaign against graffiti. Apart from the strategic value of this move, it was also in keeping with his character. A lover of trains from boyhood on, and a man with a passion for cleanliness and order, Gunn saw graffiti as a blight on the system, and he was determined to wipe it out.

But this was New York, and there were those who disagreed, arguing that graffiti was a form of art. Why was the MTA so preoccupied with graffiti when it had problems that were far more serious? Graffiti didn't endanger anyone's life, like derailments and track fires and broken-down trains. It didn't even prevent people from getting to work on time, like the practice of red-flagging damaged track instead of repairing it, a practice that sometimes reduced train speeds by as much as 75 percent.

The answer from the other side was equally vehement. Graffiti wasn't art, it was vandalism in art's clothing. And what's more, it was depressing and demoralizing.

Transit had tackled graffiti in the past, mounting expensive battles that had ended in defeat. Prison-style fences and guard dogs had been tried—but the graffiti writers cut the wire, fed the dogs, and made canvases out of the cars. At one time, the entire IRT fleet had been covered with white lacquer paint with the thought that the cars could run advertisements, creating blank surfaces that were soon covered with tags and murals.

Gunn understood that a graffiti writer's chief thrill was to see his tag circulating through the city. Short-circuit this thrill, and the temptation would be gone—this was the principle of his Clean Car Campaign. No train would be allowed to leave the yard if it had graffiti, a policy that is still in place today, and any car discovered with graffiti had to be taken out of service within twenty-four hours.

The Clean Car program was started in May of 1984. In May of 1989, the subway was finally clean.

"The first time we ran a line without graffiti, we knew we had it," Joe Hofmann, then project manager of the Clean Car Campaign, notes. "One line. Not more," he repeats with a pleased smile. "Just getting the number 4 running—we knew we had won."

The subway was turning into a success story, breaking out of its downward spiral. Once the cars and the organization were in good condition, the system turned to rehabilitating its tracks and stations. Disgruntled passengers now complained about the shutting down of stations and the rerouting of trains, but there was a new spirit in the air, and their complaints were comparatively good-natured.

The culture of the subway was changing as well, thanks to the Arts for Transit program, established in 1985, formed to oversee the art that was commissioned as part of all station rehabilitation. The design criteria for the original IRT and BRT were used to establish guidelines that would be respectful of the past, with the IRT/BRT stations done in a meld of Beaux Arts and Arts and Crafts, and the original IND lines invoking modernism. Different color palettes were developed for individual stations, affecting their overall design.

Times Square Mural © Roy Lichtenstein. Designed 1990, fabricated 1994, installed 2002. Times Square station. Commissioned and owned by MTA Arts for Transit. Courtesy of MTA Arts for Transit

Stations could be approached aesthetically now that the system was fully operational. The result? An underground museum that extended across the five boroughs, receiving millions of visitors every day. A museum that caught the viewer by surprise, flashing upon him as he sped to his destination, without asking for anything in return.

Parsons had designed the subway "with an eye to beauty as well as to its official function," and now that beauty was being restored. As the century came to an end, the subway was undergoing a renaissance.

And behind the scenes, in the vast yet closely knit world that the public rarely sees, the subway was regathering its strength, as though in preparation for the punishing trials that would mark the beginning of the new century.

CHAPTER TEN

Steel Arches

W hen William Barclay Parsons drew up his design for the subway one hundred years ago, he could never have foreseen the events of September 11, 2001. If he had been alive to witness the tragedy, he would have been desperate to inspect his tunnels. Descending into the subway, he would have seen remarkable sights: great I beams twisted into outlandish shapes, concrete ceilings sagging like pieces of wet cloth. The damage would have been appalling to him: over 575 feet of subway utterly destroyed.

If skyscrapers were "the spectacular consequence of the subway" (Parsons' phrase), they were now also the cause of spectacular damage.

A beam from 7 World Trade Center pierces the tunnel north of Vesey Street, and nothing on earth can pull it out. Tremendous wire cables are attached to it, but at the critical moment they snap like strings.

At last, the exhausted workers cut off the top of the beam, leaving the rest of it hidden under the tunnel floor. There is no way of knowing how deeply the beam is buried, or whether it will ever come to light again, once it is sealed with concrete and overlaid with track.

NYCT officials inspect Cortlandt Street station damage following the attack of September 11, 2001. Patrick Cashin, MTA photographer, NYTM

There was intense, incessant labor underground, as in the days when the subway was first being built.

As the towers fall, tons of debris land on West Broadway, causing many support beams in the tunnels there to collapse. The street and the sidewalks have little to hold them up, and they are in great danger of caving in.

Workers are ordered to fill the tunnel with concrete, enough concrete, according to the New York Times, *to cover an entire football field one foot deep. After the debris is cleared away, the concrete will have to be carved out so that a new tunnel can be built.*

As firefighters struggled to put out smoldering fires, transit workers battled against the threat of floods.

Part of "the Bathtub," a waterproof barrier that ringed the basement of the World Trade Center, is destroyed when the buildings fall, and now there is a real danger that the 1 and 9 tunnels at Chambers and Cedar Streets will be inundated by the Hudson River.

Three-foot-thick plugs made of steel and concrete are installed in the tunnels to keep the river from pouring in. Once the barrier is reinforced, these giant plugs will be torn out and demolished.

Actions and reactions, played out over a period of weeks and months, against a stark background of shock and grief. And while the system strained to adapt, engineers came from all around the world to learn what they could from the tragedy.

"For us, a disaster is a test," a Swiss engineer remarked, "and while we wish that 9/11 had never happened, the data that we are gathering here is, of course, extraordinary." Parsons' design had been put to the most extreme of tests: dozens of stories had fallen onto its roof from a height of 600 feet.

What did the engineers conclude? Many of them were amazed that the damage wasn't worse. Although the devastation was severe, there were only two areas of complete tunnel collapse around the station at Cortlandt Street. "The part of the subway that took the hardest hit was built back in the beginning of the twentieth century," Art Bethell points out. "Just imagine the amount of effort that went into the construction to withstand the impact of the twin towers falling onto it."

What was the secret of the subway's strength?

Parsons would have known the answer right away. It was the steel arches of his original design, arches that were spaced five feet apart and encased in a brick and concrete box to form the tunnels that often lay no more than five feet below the surface of the street.

Each arch possessed its own independent strength, and the fact that there were so many of them prevented the tunnels from caving in, even when individual arches were destroyed by the cruel force that suddenly bore down on them.

When plans for the rebuilding of the subway were drawn up, Parsons' design had a guiding influence. The new 1 and 9 tunnels would be based on drawings of the old IRT line, taken from the New York Transit Museum archives. With beams placed five feet apart and ties that were made of wood, the new tunnel would truly be the child of the old, born out of its ruins, perpetuating its form.

But the subway is more than the sum of its physical parts, its tunnels, stations, trains, and tracks: it is a work in progress carried out by 27,000 men and women. And whether they were operating trains up in the Bronx or assisting in the rescue operations at Ground Zero, every transit worker in the system was tested on the morning of 9/11.

At the Control Center on Jay Street, after the first plane hits, staff workers instantly swing into action. They have no time to speculate about what is unfolding before their eyes; they must remain keenly focused on the moment. Operators all across the system are instructed to bypass the vicinity of the World Trade Center. At 10:20, after the first tower falls, the staff works feverishly to halt all service.

Approximately 200,000 passengers are evacuated, 60,000 of them in the area of the World Trade Center. The nerve center of the system has absorbed a tremendous jolt, and it reacts by thrusting its passengers out of danger.

"When the building fell, I had just walked out of 7 World Trade Center," Joe Hofmann recalls, "because I had been sent down to the scene. I dove behind a car, and then I went to Chambers Street to make a call. By that time, they had already rerouted the trains.

Subway station damage from September 11, 2001, attack. Felix Candelaria, NYCT senior photographer

"Nobody had told them how to do that. They knew what to do—we had rehearsed it many times. So we didn't lose a single customer. We didn't even lose any equipment or trains."

In the dark, uncertain hours that follow, the Control Center becomes like a war room. Transit officials from the highest levels of the system join with members of the Planning Division, huddling around maps hastily posted on the walls or studying color-coded model boards that represent every station in the system.

A towable trailer fitted out with telephones and Nextels becomes Transit's headquarters at Ground Zero. This trailer becomes the entry point for the hundreds of transit workers who flock to the rescue operation.

Reports and orders flash back and forth between the trailer and the Control Center on Jay Street. The problems

Steel girder construction for new 1/9 subway line tunnel on World Trade Center site, 2002. William Coughlin, NYCT senior photographer

at Ground Zero are staggering, calling for a dizzying array of equipment and machinery: a possibility of flooding threatens to take out the entire telephone system of New York; tons of wreckage block rescue operations, concrete boulders, massive iron beams, mountains of fallout from the decimated buildings . . .

Two hours after the towers fall, a five-block-long con- voy of heavy machinery appears on the scene, dump trucks, loaders, backhoes, cranes—"you name it, we had it," one transit worker recalls—all provided by New York City Transit.

"We were the first ones to have emergency service," Hofmann notes. "And we had other things ready that peo- ple don't know about. We had a train on the E line, a hos-

pital train. And we had another train that was ready to go back and forth to Forty-second Street to bring the injured back out because the streets were too congested for the ambulances. But in reality, nobody came out. We didn't realize that at the time."

An overwhelming desire to help quickly rises up in the ranks. By five in the afternoon of 9/11, 3,500 transit workers are working side by side with policemen and firefighters, and more and more workers want to join. But Transit can't afford to have all its forces deployed in the danger-fraught environment of Ground Zero, to the bitter frustration of many transit workers. Under threat of dismissal, the workers return to their regular shifts, but many of them volunteer at the site after hours.

On Friday, September 14, outside contractors are brought in and Transit headquarters at Ground Zero are

demobilized. For the subway workers who have been
working around the clock from the very first day of the
tragedy, it is emotionally wrenching to leave the site.

"I saw things down there that I'll never forget," one
transit worker says. "The only comfort was the hope that
we could get somebody out. That's why it was so hard to
be sent away."

Weeks after the tragedy of 9/11, the Control Center was still in high gear. "There was a whole host of things that were going on," Herbert Lambert, assistant chief transportation officer of the Control Center, recalls, citing the flooding of the line from Christopher to Franklin as one of many examples, a situation that necessitated the termination of trains from Fourteenth Street down, so that the tunnels could be pumped out. "We finally started getting the system reopened piece by piece," Lambert goes on. "By November we were sort of settled in, but we were still disrupted because of suspicious powders. Initially we stopped trains. Then we developed procedures so that service was no longer shut down. Then we developed hammer teams that would respond to particular places."

As the system struggled to regain its equilibrium, the ridership underwent a crisis of confidence. Ridership dropped sharply after 9/11, but as early as October 21 National Public Radio was reporting that it was back to 98 percent of what it had been before. In a city in which tall buildings suddenly seemed terribly exposed, the underground neighborhood of the subway was still holding together.

The system had rallied mightily in the first days and weeks of the crisis, but now it was faced with the mammoth task of rebuilding. As of September 28, 2001, transit officials were saying that the 1 and 9 line from south of Chambers Street to the South Ferry station would probably take more than two years to rebuild. Apart from the 575 feet of subway that had completely collapsed, hundreds of feet of tunnel were structurally unsound. A total of 6,200 feet of subway would have to be rebuilt, and because the tunnels were choked with debris, the engineers couldn't predict when the work would actually begin, let alone when it would be finished.

In the space of one year, 1.6 million tons of wreckage were cleared away: concrete boulders, fragments of buildings, iron beams. Between March and September of 2002, a crew of thirty engineers and three hundred construction workers and employees worked around the clock to rebuild 1,400 feet of tunnel and lay 2,800 feet of track.

As of September 17, 2002, the 1 and 9 trains were running again, almost through the middle of Ground Zero to South Ferry. The Cortlandt Street station on the N and R line was reopened; the 2 and 3 trains were back on the express tracks in Manhattan. To the amazement of everyone who was paying attention, the work had been finished months before deadline and $50 million below budget.

Like children who have been sent away from a war-torn city and then brought home again, the public eagerly reclaimed its subway lines. For them, normalcy had finally been restored, but for those who had been part of the labor and the toil, nothing short of a miracle had been achieved.

"This was a cut artery in New York City and now the bleeding has stopped," said New York City Transit engineer Joel Zakoff on September 15, 2002, when the 1 and 9 line was reopened. The greatest transit system in the world was back on its feet again. "It's the phoenix rising from its ashes."

(1325) CON 2 JORALEMON
& FURMAN STS. 14-6-05

Building the Subway

Sandhog exiting the "man-lock," Furman and Joralemon Streets, Brooklyn; IRT Contract 2 line. June 1905. A "man-lock" is a pressurized chamber. One of the occupational hazards of tunnel work was a condition known as "the bends," caused by a build-up of gas bubbles in tissue. The highest pressure in a tunnel was 100 pounds per square inch. Men could work under these conditions only for half hour shifts.

The following images show rural areas in Queens, undeveloped tracts of land in the Bronx, and already developed areas of upper Manhattan on the brink of the massive transformation brought about by the building of the subway.

Roosevelt Avenue between Peartree and Morris Avenues, Queens; IRT Corona line. September 1923.

Site of Zerega Avenue station, Bronx; IRT Pelham line. May 1916.

Site of Whitlock Avenue station, Bronx; IRT Pelham line. May 1914.

122nd Street and St. Nicholas Avenue, Manhattan; IND Eighth Avenue line. 1925. Throughout the 1920s, Mayor John Hylan was one of the driving forces behind the creation of the municipally owned Independent Subway System (IND). The sign on the street marks the beginning of construction.

What was the best way of digging the subway hole in New York? The so-called cut-and-cover method, adapted from the recently constructed subway system in Budapest, was believed to be the best approach. It consisted of digging a shallow trench in which the subway construction took place. When the work was completed, the street was rebuilt over it. Though this was the most typical approach, the builders came up against many obstacles that forced them to find a variety of alternatives.

City Hall loop, Manhattan; IRT Contract 1 line. February 1902.

Chambers and Centre Streets, Manhattan; BRT Centre Street loop.
May 1908.

42nd Street and Broadway, Manhattan; IRT Contract 1 line. May 1903.

Broadway and 158th Street, Manhattan; IRT Contract 1 line. October 1900.

(378) B'WAY + 158 "ST.

Tunneling through solid rock turned subway building into a mining operation. Instead of digging a trench, workers bored dynamite holes; the foremen and the engineers set the dynamite; and excavators cleared away the spoils. In some cases, rock tunnels were created at a considerable depth from the surface. On upper Broadway, between 145th Street and Fort George Hill, workers made two deep vertical shafts and then tunneled their way northward and southward from the base of those shafts. Rock tunneling was also done on the Manhattan side of the river tunnel going to Brooklyn, as well as other areas, such as the Lexington Avenue line, in which workers used both cut-and-cover and rock tunneling.

Central Park, Manhattan; IRT Contract 1 lne. December 1902. Note the rolling platform or "traveler" in the newly excavated tunnel. This traveler, which operates on rails placed along the edges of the rock wall, is used to build the concrete sidewalls.

(2491) CENTRAL PARK 12-8-1902

Rubble after blowing a charge, 181st Street and Broadway, Manhattan; IRT
Contract 1 line. March 1901.

OPPOSITE: Sixth Avenue around 34th Street, Manhattan; IND Sixth Avenue
line. October 1938. Construction in this area was extremely complicated
because of already existing lines—the Hudson Tubes, the Broadway BMT
line, the 32nd and 33rd Street tubes of Pennsylvania Station, not to mention
the Sixth Avenue El.

Powder shanty for storing explosives, Union Square Park near 15th Street and Union Square West, Manhattan; BRT 14th Street Canarsie line. January 1917.

RIGHT: Lexington Avenue between 96th and 103rd Streets, Manhattan; IRT Lexington Avenue line. February 1913.

(2957) R5 S11 LEX AVE.

Lexington Avenue between 96th and 103rd Streets, Manhattan; IRT Lexington
Avenue line. February 1912.

R5 511.
(871) STA. 359 +05.
LEX. AVE. 2-15-1912

In the midst of the first phase of excavation, the engineers and contractors organized the workforce, procured equipment—pneumatic tools, hoists, drills, pumps, concrete mixers, and riveters—and arranged for the material needed for the actual construction of the subway.

Park Row, Manhattan; IRT Contract 1 line. November 1902.

(2865) PARK ROW   11-13-1902

Fourth Avenue and 20th Street, Manhattan; IRT Contract 1 line. June 1901.

103rd Street and Lexington Avenue, Manhattan; IRT Lexington Avenue line.
March 1913. Unstable rock required continuous girders to support the decking. The long wooden columns visible in the image are supporting the girders.

OPPOSITE: Kenmare Street between Mulberry and Mott Streets, Manhattan;
BRT Centre Street loop. June 1908.

(666) Con 9-0-4 MULBERRY
-MOTT ST 6-5-1908

42nd Street and Broadway, Manhattan; IRT Contract 1 line. July 1903.

Trimming rock with horizontally positioned air drill, Sixth Avenue between
Canal and West Fourth Streets, near Spring Street, Manhattan; IND Eighth
Avenue line. February 1928.

All aspects of subway construction required coordination. For example, the excavation and the construction work proceeded more efficiently if the rock that was blasted out of the tunnel hole could also be ground up and combined with cement to make the concrete to pour foundations for the subway track. Removing the "spoils" was an important piece of the puzzle of subway construction. There were several different ways of getting rid of the spoils: mules, shovels, and hoists.

Trinity Place, Manhattan; BRT Broadway line. September 1913. The columns shown here are temporary supports, providing just enough room for the excavation cars and their spoils.

(3608) R. S. S. 1. TRINITY. PL.
STA. 25+41. 9.9.1913

Teams of horses excavating spoils, Ashland Place and Fulton Street, Brooklyn; BRT Fourth Avenue line. January 1911. The Brooklyn Academy of Music is visible in the upper left-hand corner.

RIGHT: Central Park around 60th Street, Manhattan; BRT Broadway line. October 1915.

CENTRAL FORK
10-6-1915

Church Street, between Thomas and Worth Streets, Manhattan; IND Eighth Avenue line. October 1927.

Lexington Avenue between 94th and 95th Streets, Manhattan; IRT Lexington Avenue line. February 1913. The shovel on the right is depositing spoils into the "battleship" on the left. Battleships were buckets placed on small cars with cradles shaped to fit them. The cars were then rolled down narrow-gauge track to a point where they could be hauled upgrade by small stationary hoisting machines. The buckets could then be hoisted to the surface by derricks.

130th Street and St. Nicholas Avenue, Manhattan; IND Eighth Avenue line.
June 1925.

Duane Street, Manhattan; BRT Centre Street loop. July 1909.

14th Street, Manhattan; BRT 14th Street Canarsie line. August 1919.

Near DeKalb Avenue station, Brooklyn; BMT Brighton line.
May 1919.

Material shaft, 60th Street tunnel, BRT Broadway line. November 1917.

OPPOSITE: 14th Street between Fourth Avenue and Irving Place, Manhattan;
BRT 14th Street Canarsie line. December 1916.

OVERLEAF: 16. Fourth Avenue, between 9th and Union Streets, Brooklyn;
BRT Fourth Avenue line. February 1912.

BOOTH & FLINN co.
GENERAL CONTRACTORS
NEW YORK · PITTSBURGH
PUBLIC SERVICE COMMISSION
FIRST DISTRICT

STEINW

URAL
CIGARETTES

PIANOS

RESTAURANT

(1001) R851-14" ST.
12-19-1916.

Because the subway was often built close to the surface of the street, its construction involved the relocation of underground pipes and ducts. Sewers, water and gas mains, steam pipes, pneumatic tubes, and electric conduits were tightly packed together just beneath the trolley tracks, which took up the streets. The first phase of subway construction entailed rerouting and rebuilding this maze of existing pipes and structures, often without the benefit of utility line maps.

105th Street and Lexington Avenue, Manhattan; IRT Lexington Avenue line. June 1913.

(3358) R.S.S.11. STA. 382+66
105. ST. + LEX. AVE
6.12.1913

Relocating utility lines, Broadway and Murray Street, Manhattan; BRT
Broadway line. March 1915.

Work on sewer line, 71st Street and Broadway, Manhattan; IRT Contract 1
line. December 1902.

Spring and Elm (now Lafayette) Streets, Manhattan; IRT Contract 1 line.
November 1902.

125th Street and Lenox Avenue, Manhattan; IRT Contract 1 line. April 1904.

Siphon form for pouring concrete, Fourth Avenue, Brooklyn; IRT Brooklyn line. July 1915.

OPPOSITE: Construction of new sewer line, Lafayette Street, Brooklyn; IRT Contract 2 line. November 1905.

(1646) Con. 2 Lafayette
St. 11-74-1905

Among the many lines that had to be rerouted, the gas lines were some of the most hazardous. Because of the danger of leaks and explosions, many gas mains had to be rerouted overhead and across streets. Other cast-iron gas mains that remained under decking had to be properly vented and sometimes even monitored by guards.

Gas bypass on Chambers Street, west of Church Street, Manhattan; IND Eighth Avenue line. January 1928.

OVERLEAF: 110th Street and Cathedral Circle, Manhattan; IND Eighth Avenue line. May 1928. Note the Ninth Avenue El in the upper right-hand corner. The sharp bend in the track as it curved around Cathedral Circle was known as "Suicide Curve," site of many tragedies.

(1296) CON.2. EXCHANGE
PL. BWAY 6.7.1905

Overhead steel gas bypass across Sixth Avenue at Minetta Lane, Manhattan;
IND Eighth Avenue line. November 1927. Temporary steel pipes for bypassing
sewer are shown on lower left, and sheeting for the sump is visible in the cut.

OPPOSITE: Exchange Place and Broadway, Manhattan; IRT Contract 2 line.
June 1905. The gas line to the left is raised because of the danger of leaks
and explosions. The larger pipe that remains in the trench is a water main.

The construction of the subway line on upper Broadway had to accommodate vehicular traffic as well as two electric trolley car lines. This was accomplished by building temporary contractors' bridges for each track, with each bridge consisting of a pair of timber trusses that were braced high enough together to let a trolley car pass below.

View north from Columbus Circle, 59th Street, Manhattan; IRT Contract 1 line. July 1901. Broadway is on the left; Central Park West, to the right.

96th Street and Broadway, Manhattan; IRT Contract 1 line. July 1903.

OPPOSITE: Looking south from Broadway at the intersection of 72nd Street and Amsterdam Avenue, Manhattan; IRT Contract 1 line. October 1902.

(2254) 72ˢᵗ ST. + BᵂAY
10-9-1902

Timbering was a method of supporting the street surface while tunnel construction took place below. The regular system of timbering involved cross-bracing, rangers, and posts. There were two general types of timbering—one for earth and one for rock. With earth excavation, side sheeting had to be put in place to prevent the earth from spilling and weakening the area around it. With rock excavation, a clear working space and additional supports were needed to safeguard against disaster. Blasting operations could trigger slides in the rock, which was already very unstable in places. The following images show the structures that supported the temporary decking that covered the street.

Inspector examining water seepage, St. Nicholas Avenue between 141st and 145th Streets, Manhattan; IND Eighth Avenue line. December 1927. Timber and concrete were used to support this wall.

Bowling Green, Manhattan; IRT Contract 2 line. June 1904.

Broadway between 73rd and 74th Streets, Manhattan; IRT Contract 1 line.
November 1902. Because Broadway is a boulevard divided by a mall, the
central cut could be left open longer than in other areas.

Broadway and 87th Street, Manhattan; IRT Contract 1 line. June 1901.
Timbering became more complicated when rock and earth were combined.

OPPOSITE: Duane Street, Manhattan; BRT Centre Street loop. July 1911.

(1341) 9-0-1-DUANE. Sr.
7-31-1911

Rock wall bracing, Lexington Avenue between 102nd and 103rd Streets,
Manhattan; IRT Lexington Avenue line. June 1914.

St. Nicholas Avenue between 145th and 146th Streets, Manhattan; IND
Eighth Avenue line. April 1928.

West side of Ashland Place, looking north from Lafayette Avenue, Brooklyn;
BRT Fourth Avenue line. January 1911. In the background is the Majestic
Theater.

Ashland Place and Lafayette Avenue, Brooklyn; BRT Fourth Avenue line.
1911. The same site, several months later.

Narrow-gauge excavation tracks, 60th Street tunnel, from Manhattan to
Queens; BRT Broadway line. January 1917.

Near East Houston Street, Manhattan; IND Houston Street line. April 1931.

The following images, taken at or above the surface level, show the decking that covered subway trenches.

Great Jones and Elm (now Lafayette) Streets, Manhattan; Contract 1 line. August 1901.

Union Square, Manhattan; IRT Contract 1 line. February 1903.

Union Square, Manhattan; IRT Contract 1 line. October 1903. Eight months
later, the decking along the east side of Fourth Avenue is in place.

Centre and Pearl Streets, Manhattan; BRT Centre Street loop. October 1912.

OPPOSITE: Exchange Place and Broadway, Manhattan; IRT Contract 2 line. November 1904. Wooden decking and a rerouted gas line are on either side of trolley tracks.

(816) Con 2, EXCHANGE. PL
9 BWAY   11-15-1904

Delancey Street, Manhattan; BRT Centre Street loop. June 1909. This image shows work prior to decking.

(1201)CON.9-8-4. BENT 34
6.25.1909

Seventh Avenue and 42nd Street, Manhattan; IRT Seventh Avenue line.
September 1914.

OPPOSITE: 23rd Street and Fourth Avenue, Manhattan; IRT Contract 1 line.
May 1903.

Bridge and Fulton Streets, Brooklyn; IRT Contract 2 line. June 1907. Notice
the sign, which reads, "The care of this street is not within the jurisdiction of
the Borough President. All complaints should be lodged with the Board of
the Rapid Transit Commission."

Fourth Avenue and 37th Street, Brooklyn; BRT Fourth Avenue line. January 1910.

Fourth Avenue and 37th Street, Brooklyn; BRT Fourth Avenue line. June 1911.

The following images show construction work in the large open trench.

Sixth Avenue, looking north from White Street near Church Street, Manhattan; IND Eighth Avenue line. August 1928.

(2062) R101 53
CHURCH ST.
NORTH OF
WHITE St.
8-8-28

Astor Place looking west, 8th Street and Fourth Avenue, Manhattan, IRT
Contract 1 line. August 1903. The brick wall and conduit (on the left) are
being built along the concrete track bed.

(3670) 9.St & 4ᵗʰ Ave
8-18-1909

Astor Place, looking south, 9th Street and Fourth Avenue, Manhattan; IRT
Contract 1 line. August 1903. In the foreground, workers are waterproofing the
concrete surface with tar, a material that was soon phased out because it led to
overheating in the tunnels. In the background, the track is being laid out. The
Cooper Union is in the upper left-hand corner.

Site of Bryant Park, 42nd Street between Fifth and Sixth Avenues,
Manhattan; IRT Queensborough line. April 1924. In the background is
the Sixth Avenue El.

Sixth Avenue, looking south at York Street toward Lispenard Street,
Manhattan; IND Eighth Avenue line. January 1929.

Several methods of construction were used to build the subway tunnels for the original Contract 1 line. The most common was the flat-roofed structure with steel I beams on the top and sides. The materials used to build this type of tunnel included concrete, crushed stone, felt, and asphalt. Conditions varied widely along different parts of the route, requiring different approaches. For example, concrete-lined tunnels cast from large wooden forms were used in both the rock tunneling at Fort George and in the open-cut work on upper Broadway.

Constructing wooden forms for casting concrete, Broadway and 158th Street, Manhattan; IRT Contract 1 line. May 1901.

5-15-1901
(1017) BWAY 158 ST.

41st Street and Park Avenue, Manhattan; IRT Contract 1 line. November 1903. Half of the original Contract 1 line was constructed using steel I beams, which served as sidewall columns, and horizontal ceiling beams. Another quarter of the line was built as a concrete-lined arch tunnel. This image shows the convergence of the two methods of tunnel construction.

103rd Street and Broadway, Manhattan; IRT Contract 1 line. November 1903. The concrete arch of the lower tunnel is providing the support on which the upper level of track can be laid.

138th Street and Broadway, Manhattan; IRT Contract 1 line. April 1903.

60th Street and Fourth Avenue, Brooklyn; BRT Fourth Avenue line. February 1915. Fluted steel walls are being surfaced with concrete. The irregularly laid ties and uneven track indicate that this is a temporary line used in construction for moving material.

60th Street Tunnel from Manhattan to Queens; BRT Broadway line.
September 1917.

Unloading concrete buckets, Manhattan; IND Eighth Avenue line.
October 1928.

Car clearance template, Central Park West between 96th and 103rd Streets, Manhattan; IND Eighth Avenue line. December 1928.

OPPOSITE: Near 42nd Street and Lexington Avenue, Manhattan; IRT Lexington Avenue line. July 1919. The curve in the track indicates the turn from Park toward Lexington Avenue, as part of the extension from the original Contract 1 line.

(587)R4331-STA
209+92-7-29-19.

A concrete-lined section of the Fort George tunnel, 151st Street and
Broadway, Manhattan; IRT Contract 1 line. July 1903.

(3577) 151 St 4 BWAY
7-28-1903

In the early years of tunnel construction, timber supports used to shore up nearby buildings and elevated train tracks became a familiar sight.

Park Avenue, Manhattan; IRT Contract 1 line. March 1902. On March 19, 1902, a severe rock slide occurred in the east tunnel beneath Park Avenue, disturbing the surface of the street and causing parts of several house walls to collapse. This image, taken a few days later, documents the timbering that was needed to secure the weakened facades.

LUNCH ROOM
105 ROELGERS SON'S
AUGUSTINER BEER

WINES

CABINET MAKER

WHISKIES JOHN

(288b) HOWARD & ELM St

Centre Street, Manhattan; BRT Centre Street loop. October 1909.

OPPOSITE: Shoring during building demolition, Howard and Elm (now
Lafayette) Streets, Manhattan; IRT Contract 1 line. March 1903.

Fulton Street and Flatbush Avenue, Brooklyn; IRT Contract 2 line. April 1905.

Fulton Street and Flatbush Avenue, Brooklyn; IRT Contract 2 line. September 1907. Buildings were not the only structures that needed support as the subway was being constructed underground. The wooden decking that replaced the cobblestones and the timber A-frames supporting the elevated tracks are signs of tunnel construction.

(2200) FULTON ST.
CON.2   7-16-07

Timber A-frames around elevated line columns, Fulton Street, Brooklyn, IRT Contract 2 line. July 1907.

A great effort was made to carry on this monumental construction project underground without interrupting the life of the city, but there were failures. The following images show cave-ins, shortly after the fact.

Nostrand Avenue, Brooklyn; IRT Flatbush line. July 1916.

S(8)R 29 SE
TA 200 + 20
7-14-1916

Fourth Avenue, Bay Ridge, Brooklyn; BRT Fourth Avenue line. June 1914.

38th Street and Broadway, Manhattan; BRT Broadway line. September 1915.

Flatbush and St. Marks Avenues, Brooklyn; IRT Brooklyn line. December 1914. This image documents a collapse of decking due to a break in the St. Marks Avenue sewer at the northeast corner of Flatbush Avenue.

933)R12 SI. FLATBUSH - ST. MARKS AVES.
TA·33+00.   12-21-14.

Before the cave-in, St. Felix Street and Hanson Place, Brooklyn; BRT
Brighton line. March 1916. Notice the name of the business on the first floor
of the corner building: "Subway Shirt Hospital."

St. Felix Street and Hanson Place, Brooklyn; BRT Brighton line. April 1917.
The face of the storefront has been shorn away.

Nos. 874 and 878 Eighth Avenue, between 50th and 59th Streets,
Manhattan; IND Eighth Avenue line. February 1928.

OPPOSITE: View from below street level, Eighth Avenue between 50th and
59th Streets, Manhattan; IND Eighth Avenue line. February 1928.

(1233) R 102 S5
874+878-8
7-16-28

STYLE PLUS COMFORT - FOR WOMEN

PHYSICAL CULTURE SHOE

PHYSICAL CULTURE SHOE

SOLD BY JOHN F. VACCARA
36½ BROADWAY NEAR 149 ST

(2823) R18-544
ST. NICHOLAS-AVE 147-148-ST
STA 1357+10 5-25-28

St. Nicholas Avenue between 147th and 148th Streets, Manhattan; IND Washington Heights line. May 1928.

Several dramatically different methods were used to construct the river tunnels that connected Manhattan to the Bronx, Brooklyn, and Queens. Some of these images show the construction of the Lexington Avenue tunnel under the Harlem River, which extended the IRT Lexington Avenue line from upper Manhattan to the Bronx. First, cast-iron tubes were fabricated; then fully built sections of the tunnel structure were floated into the Harlem River. Once the tubes were positioned over a predredged site, they were filled with water, sunk into place, and secured.

Other images document the construction of the river tunnel that stretched from lower Manhattan to Brooklyn. This tunnel was part of the IRT Contract 2 line and marked the first subway route into Brooklyn. A large section of the tunnel consisted of two cast-iron tubes, constructed of circular cast-iron plates that were bolted together and then reinforced. The tubes were constructed under the riverbed by means of the shield method, which involved using an enormous circular shield driven by 2,000 tons of hydraulic pressure to cut through the earth. As the shield pushed forward, cast-iron sections of the tube were bolted together.

Building the wooden lining into which concrete will be poured, 152nd Street and Harlem River, Bronx; IRT Lexington Avenue line. July 1913.

(3479) R. 5. S. 14. 152. S⊤
HARLEM. RIVER
7.11.1913

Bolting the pieces of the tubes together, 152nd Street and Harlem River, Bronx; IRT Lexington Avenue line. June 1913.

Towing the tunnel tubes into place, Harlem River between Madison Avenue and the New York City Bridge, August 1913. Bulkheads kept water out of tunnel tubes. Additional buoyancy tubes were connected to the top. When the tunnel tubes were positioned, all the tubes were gradually filled with water, which caused the tunnel tubes to sink into place.

152nd Street and Harlem River, Bronx; IRT Lexington Avenue line. July 1913.

In the emergency lock of a bulkhead, shaft #1, Clark Street tunnel, East River; IRT Seventh Avenue line.
April 1916.

Plates for tunnel, near Warehouse no. 66, Furman and Joralemon Streets, Brooklyn; IRT Contract 2 line. February 1904.

RIGHT: Battery Park, Manhattan; IRT Contract 2 line. Circa 1907. The plates were bolted together to form a section of tube.

Constructing the river tunnel tube, piece by piece, Battery Park, Manhattan;
IRT Contract 2 line. June 1907.

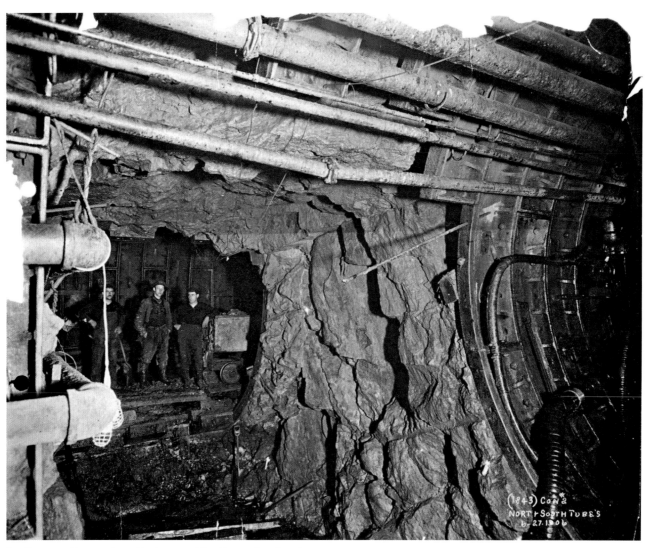

East River tunnel between lower Manhattan and Brooklyn, north and south
tubes; IRT Contract 2 line. June 1906.

Work gang caulking and tightening bolts on Manhattan ring of East River tube; IRT Contract 2 line. October 1907.

Workers hoisting section of East River tunnel ring into place, Joralemon
Street, Brooklyn; IRT Contract 2 line. June 1903.

14th Street and Avenue D, Manhattan; BRT 14th Street Canarsie line.
November 1916.

14th Street and Avenue D, Manhattan; BRT 14th Street Canarsie line. November 1916.

14th Street and Avenue D, Manhattan, BRT 14th Street Canarsie line. November 1916.

Inside ends of locks, Fulton Street tunnel, East River; IND line. March 1929. The small upper lock allows workers access to the heading, while the lower lock on the right allows dump cars to be pulled from the heading to the shaft.

RIGHT: Work gang exiting through a lock, Fulton Street tunnel; IND line. May 1929.

The city's elevated lines were notorious for congestion and noise, one of the many reasons why New York badly needed an underground system. However, the projected cost of doing all of the work below street level was prohibitive. In the end, the realization of the subway system depended on a compromise: in order to reach the far-flung districts of the outer boroughs, elevated extensions would be built in as yet undeveloped areas of the Bronx, Queens, and Brooklyn, and some of the existing elevated lines would be incorporated into the new system.

The following images show construction of new elevated structures as extensions of the underground subway lines in Manhattan, the Bronx, and Queens.

Roosevelt Avenue and 35th Street, Queens; IRT Corona line. October 1914.

East Side viaduct, Westchester Avenue, Bronx; IRT Contract 1 line.
October 1903.

Constructing the Manhattan Valley viaduct, 125th Street and Broadway,
Manhattan; IRT Contract 1 line. July 1903. Instead of tunneling underground,
the planners decided to design a 2,174-foot-long viaduct that would cross
between 125th and 133rd Streets in Manhattan Valley.

133rd Street and Broadway, Manhattan; IRT Contract 1 line. August 1902.

Dyckman Street station, Manhattan; IRT Contract 1 line. October 1905. The Kingsbridge Generating Plant for streetcar lines of the Third Avenue railway system is visible in the background.

207th Street station, Manhattan; IRT Contract 1 line. June 1906. Stations along the elevated portions of the Contract 1 line were designed by Heins and LaFarge. Their station designs echoed the Victorian designs of the elevated railway.

232nd Street and Broadway, Bronx; IRT Contract 1 line. May 1907. Workers on either side of the rail line are digging out footings for the columns that will support the elevated subway.

242nd Street station, Bronx; IRT Contract 1 line. April 1908.

242nd Street station, Bronx; IRT Contract 1 line. May 1925.

241st Street station, Bronx; IRT White Plains Road line. August 1924.

(122) R36 + 3753 QUEENS BOULEVARD
BENT 155 · 11-25-1913

Queens Boulevard, Queens; IRT Corona line. November 1913. When an
elevated line was to cross or traverse an important boulevard, special
attention was paid to the appearance of these structures. Such was the case
of the elevated line that ran above Queens Boulevard. This design called for
an ornamental structure of reinforced concrete.

Queens Boulevard, Roosevelt Avenue, and Gosman Street, Queens; IRT
Corona line. November 1914.

Whenever possible, the planners of the original system tried to take advantage of natural light, which could enter the stations through vault lights. This was possible because many stations were very close to the street surface.

The problem with air was more complicated. Even though the planners made provisions for proper ventilation of the subway, the combination of the heat generated by the trains and the crowds of passengers squeezing into the cars made the riding conditions quite unpleasant, especially in the summer. (This may be one of the reasons that the elevated extensions of the subway that were part of the Dual Contract System were advertised as "fresh air" lines.)

Laying in glass vault lights, City Hall loop, Manhattan; IRT Contract 1 line. June 1902.

Fulton Street and Broadway, Manhattan; IRT Contract 2 line. March 1905.

OPPOSITE: Bryant Park, Manhattan; IRT Contract 1 line. November 1906. After the first summer of the subway's operation, it became clear that something had to be done about the heat. Different solutions were tried, from installing fans on pillars to cutting out station lights at night, to putting in a water cooling system at the Brooklyn Bridge station. Several improvements were introduced during Contract 2 line construction. The first was to install partition walls between tracks, which functioned as vents. The second was to install louvered ventilation chambers with gratings that would allow air to vent out.

The original planners of the subway understood that in order
for this monumental project to be embraced by the public, it
had to run efficiently and be properly maintained. But in
addition to utility, the structures had to be designed with "a
view to the beauty of their appearance." Architects Heins and
LaFarge were brought in to decorate the raw brick walls and
ceilings of the forty-nine stations of the Contract 1 subway.
After establishing certain standard features for all of the
stations, Heins and LaFarge added mosaic wall treatments
to give each station its own identity, along with
individualized color schemes and a variety of other details—
cornices, garlands, cartouches, flat pilasters, Greek frets, etc.

Heins and LaFarge were also responsible for the design of the
subway entry and exit kiosks that were constructed for the
original stations. Like the cut-and-cover method of tunnel
construction, these steel and glass kiosks were adapted from
the Hungarian subway plan, which, in turn, had been
adapted from Hungarian summer houses.

The initial investment in the appearance of the subway
helped to win the public's support. But as the now popular
subway system expanded, the amount of money spent on its
visual appearance declined.

City Hall station, Manhattan; Contract 1 line. March 1904. With its
impressive use of vaulting and leaded glass, the City Hall station was the
jewel in the subway's crown.

TICKETS

(4646) CITY HALL
3.31.1904.

Entrance kiosk, City Hall station, Manhattan; Contract 1 line. Circa 1904.

Kiosks, Brooklyn Bridge station, Manhattan; Contract 1 line. Circa 1950. The Brooklyn Bridge station became the terminus for the Lexington Avenue local train when the old City Hall station was removed from service. Rounded kiosk roofs indicated entrances. Angled roofs indicated exits.

South Ferry station, Manhattan; Contract 2 line. Circa 1905. Tickets were purchased for 5 cents at ticket booths (far right). A station attendant (center) took these tickets and put them into a ticket chopper.

Awning-style subway entrance, Centre and Canal Streets, Manhattan; BRT
Centre Street loop. August 1914.

OPPOSITE: Bleecker Street station, Manhattan; IRT Contract 1 line. Circa
1904. At twenty of these original stations, extensive use of vault lights to
supply natural light to the stations minimized the need for electric light
fixtures, seen along the top of the wall. It is interesting to note that while the
source of power for the lights was independent from the power that ran the
subway, the lights could be switched to track power in case of an
emergency.

116th Street station, Manhattan; IRT Contract 1 line. 1904. This control
house, located in the center island of Broadway near Columbia University,
was torn down in 1968.

86th Street station, Manhattan; IRT Contract 1 line. Circa 1904.

96th Street station, Manhattan; IRT Contract 1 line. Circa 1904. This image shows the outer platform for the 96th Street station. The platform is no longer in use. This was one of the few stations where passengers could exit from both sides of the train.

23rd Street station, Manhattan; IRT Contract 1 line. June 1904. The steps to
the left led directly to a gallery in which one could walk into the basement
entrances of a row of shops.

125th Street station, Manhattan, IRT Lexington Avenue line. Undated.

Canal Street and Broadway, Manhattan; BMT Broadway line. March 1929. The octagonal light fixture was a trademark of the BMT line.

Ninth Avenue station, Brooklyn; BRT West End line. November 1915.

(3480) R II B 2
77 ST. STATION
1-14-1916

77th Street station, Brooklyn; BRT Fourth Avenue line. January 1916. This station entrance was originally built as part of the Triborough Plan, which employed a different architect to design the stations.

OVERLEAF: Bleecker and Lafayette Streets, Manhattan; IRT Contract 1 line. April 1960. An exit and entrance kiosk on the downtown side of the station. This image was taken shortly before these historic structures were torn down, a process that began in the late 1950s. It was said that they posed a danger for pedestrian and vehicular traffic because they obstructed vision.